# HEALING
# THE
# DOWNSIZED
# ORGANIZATION

ALSO BY DELORESE AMBROSE

*Leadership: The Journey Inward*

# HEALING

## *the*

# DOWNSIZED

# ORGANIZATION

—◆—

## DELORESE AMBROSE, ED.D.

*Harmony Books*

*New York*

*For my mother,*
*who taught me about the*
*healing qualities of work.*

Copyright © 1996 by Delorese Ambrose, Ed.D.

Published by Harmony Books, a division of Crown Publishers, Inc., 201 East 50th Street, New York, New York, 10022.

Member of the Crown Publishing Group.

Random House, Inc. New York, Toronto, London, Sydney, Auckland

http://www.randomhouse.com/

HARMONY and colophon are trademarks of Crown Publishers, Inc.

Printed in the United States of America

Library of Congress Cataloging-in-Publication Data

available upon request

ISBN 0-517-70499-4
10 9 8 7 6 5 4 3 2 1
First Edition

# CONTENTS

## Part III: CHARTING THE FUTURE

# ACKNOWLEDGMENTS

This book is a collaborative effort, for it taps the collective wisdom of all whose experiences and ideas have intersected with my own. Adrienne Ingrum, my editor, provided patient, visionary guidance and encouraged me to allow my voice to inform my writing. Her belief in the possibility of good news as fit to print made this book possible. Members of downsized organizations made an invaluable contribution by sharing their stories willingly and openly. Special thanks to John Turner and Eugene Pocci at Copperweld, Madelyn Ross and Edwina Kaikai at the *Pittsburgh Post-Gazette*, Mary Kay Loughran at Children's Hospital of Pittsburgh, Bill McDonough and Norm Mitchell at General Electric Appliances, and Bruce Leslie at Onondaga Community College.

My incredible inner circle of best friends and consulting associates is at the center of this work: Mary Gail Biebel, Kevin Covington, Richard Friend, Wendy Hardman, Jackie Heidelberg, Douglas Ligons, Peter Madsen, Danna Owczarzak, Diana Parris, and Sheila Washington. You are really special to me. I could not have written this book without your generous affection, your exemplary professionalism, and your willingness to shepherd the firm's vision and activities while I focused on my writing.

Cathleen McGrath, my teaching assistant, research assistant, sounding board, proofreader, and cheerleader—your contributions have been selfless and invaluable. Harry Pickens, my dear friend—you fired my imagination with great references and sage advice. Your genius was a wellspring of inspiration. Finally, my son Christopher Tomlinson and his fiancée, Lillian Lockley, rescued this book from the grips of a computer virus—twice. Thanks!

*Part I*

—⚏—

# THE DEATH
# OF THE
# ORGANIZATION MAN

# INTRODUCTION

The year was 1985. I was attending a national management conference to learn more about current thinking in business. The concept of total quality management (TQM) had heated up and was spreading like wildfire. Everyone was talking about "participatory management," "driving decision making further down the organization," "customer-focused approaches," "getting it right the first time, every time," and "conformance to standards." "Downsizing" and "rightsizing" were the new buzzwords, along with "empowerment" and "paradigm shifts."

Then came the highlight of the conference for me: the luncheon keynote speaker. I no longer remember his name, but I'll never forget the opening remarks of this highly controversial, self-made millionaire executive-turned-management-guru. "Mark my words," he began, "downsizing and restructuring will go down in history as the greatest management fiasco of our time." He went on to paint dramatic scenarios of broken promises, lost trust, eroded loyalties, growing cynicism, and diminished productivity. He spoke of short-term gains followed by waning profitability in the long run. He warned that employees' stress levels would escalate as their morale level and creativity plummeted. He concluded that this would eventually lead to poor quality and dissatisfied customers.

Since that conference, over 3.5 million jobs have been eradicated in Fortune 500 companies alone, as wave after wave of layoffs occur, often within the same company. Employees today are painfully aware that no one is immune from the sweeping epidemic of layoffs. Employers are downsizing in areas that were once sacred—literally. I began a recent speech with the comment "Workforce reductions are a reality in virtually every sector." A woman in the front row of the auditorium raised her hand almost immediately. "Not *virtually* every organization," she corrected me. "I just came from a meeting with a group of priests who've been laid off by the diocese. Five years ago, I'd have found that unimaginable!" The audience chuckled uncomfortably, but the point had been made.

In many ways, the management guru's words were prophetic. A 1994 American Management Association (AMA) survey reports that roughly half of the firms that have downsized since January 1989 saw an increase in operating profits following the cuts but that only slightly more than one-third of these companies realized productivity gains. Concerning the impact on the surviving workforce, the same study concludes that "time does little to heal the surest effect of downsizing, a negative impact on employee morale."

The epidemic of layoffs sweeping through the last two decades of the twentieth century continues, leaving its pockmarks on both those who lose their jobs and those who remain behind—for the moment. Admittedly, an increasing number of displaced employees go on to more healthy situations, having found ways to seize the momentum of crisis to create new work opportunities for themselves. But statistics show that more than 50 percent of those who become unemployed because of layoffs remain so a year later. Those who find work often end up in lower paying positions. Some of them never fully recover, and many are swept up in multiple layoffs, moving from one downsizing company to another. Much has been written about the plight of these obvious victims of downsizing who have their livelihoods summarily snatched from them.

Very little has been written about the less obvious victims—

those who remain in the downsizing, restructuring organization waiting anxiously for the ax to fall again. Dubbed "survivors," they find little comfort in the fact that they were spared the cuts. Betrayed by the myth of a job for life, these survivors, like the casualties of layoffs, experience the trauma of loss. They must forfeit the vestiges of job security as they endure the physical and mental stress of working smarter, harder, longer, and leaner in an organization that may itself be in crisis. Like displaced workers, employee survivors and survivor managers must deal with the nagging side effects of despair, anger, depression, and insecurity. This is a book about the ailing survivors of downsizing and about the emerging strategies for healing the personal and organizational self after the cuts.

Just a few years ago we associated layoffs with the plight of blue-collar steelworkers and underpaid coal miners fallen victims to mill closings in the wake of global competition and new technology. Now downsizing sweeps through business, industry, government, academia, and the not-for-profit sector, claiming workers regardless of their job classification, educational background, or years of seniority. No longer are layoffs the side effect of plant closings or bankrupt businesses; they have also become the prescription for continued wellness in healthy proactive organizations as well. Such organizations, with a strategic eye to the future, embrace downsizing in anticipation of growing competition and escalating costs. But cutting costs to reduce overhead and increase profits invariably means cutting flesh.

## THE DEATH OF THE ORGANIZATION MAN

In 1956 William H. Whyte coined the term "organization man" to describe the typical employee of that period. He was most likely male, white, and the financial head of a household that included a wife and children. Whether he worked as a union laborer or as a manager, he turned over his economic well-being, social life, and loyalty to the organization in exchange for security—a job for life. Clearly, this pact has been broken in the modern corporation.

Today, the typical employee is just as likely to be female as male. He or she is either a single head of a household or is raising children in a dual-career arrangement. Gone is the promise of a job for life. Gone are the expectations of a nine to five job. Today's worker either logs longer and longer hours or is seeking a flexible work schedule that allows for the integration of family and work needs.

The demise of the organization man can be traced to several social and economic trends. Whatever the cause, the fatal blow is most likely "survivor sickness," an epidemic of insecurity, mistrust, and work-related stress affecting the men and women left to run downsized organizations. Restoring health in today's organizations requires a new set of values, practices, and skills from employees and employers alike. This book will attempt to stimulate dialogue about downsizing survivors and survivor managers and about what it takes for both groups to create healthy organizations in the aftermath of loss and radical change.

Chapter 1, "The Drama of Downsizing," provides a fictionalized account of a senior manager, his colleagues, and his employees as the rapids of corporate change force him to navigate layoffs in two companies over the course of less than two years. Many of you will identify with these people as they encounter what management consultant Peter Vaill labels "permanent white water."

Chapter 2, "The Survivor's Challenge," reminds us that in many cases the unintended victims of downsizing are the so-called survivors. This chapter examines the survivor syndrome: the feelings of loss, anxiety, anger, insecurity, mistrust, and stress experienced by employees in downsized organizations, as well as the clash of personal and organizational needs that survivors must resolve in this age of reengineering and reinventing. I suggest that employer and employee are locked in a codependent relationship that must be renegotiated if organizations are to heal themselves.

Chapter 3, "The Manager's Challenge," addresses the dilemmas of surviving managers and explains why they must first heal themselves and then attend to the other survivors so that the organization itself can heal. After reviewing the mistakes made by the manager in the case presented in chapter 1, I examine what successful survivor managers do. This chapter sets the stage and lays out the criteria for assessing the real-life success stories that follow in chapters 4 through 8.

Chapter 4, "The Copperweld Case," showcases Copperweld, the world's largest producer of bimetallic wire products, and its successes in shedding old businesses and in diversifying and revitalizing its core business. Chapter 5 "The *Pittsburgh Post-Gazette* Case," features the story of a dramatic merger of two formerly competing newspapers, the *Pittsburgh Press* and *Post-Gazette*, in which the smaller of the two papers bought the larger one following a bitter eight-month strike. The resulting downsizing and restructuring is an interesting story of journalistic grit, grieving committees, and the role of crisis in the healing process. Chapter 6, "The Onondaga Community College Case," which profiles an educational institution located in Syracuse, New York, offers a look at a growing trend: downsizing and restructuring in academia. Chapter 7, "The General Electric Appliances Case," the story of a manufacturing business located in Louisville, Kentucky, shows how a Fortune 500 company successfully achieved the healing of union-management rifts during a downsizing and restructuring effort. Chapter 8, "The Children's Hospital of Pittsburgh Case," explores downsizing and reengineering in the rapidly changing health care industry.

Chapter 9, "Attending to Other Side Effects," identifies five critical issues that managers must attend to as they attempt to revitalize and heal their transforming organizations: low employee morale, the ethical quandaries of downsizing, valuing and managing diversity, managing in the dark, and healing the labor-management rift. Finally, chapter 10, "Charting a New Employee/Employer Contract," offers prescriptions for redefining work, revitalizing people, and restoring the downsized organization to a healthier state.

## WHAT IS A DOWNSIZED ORGANIZATION?

Throughout this book "downsizing" is used broadly to refer to (1) the strategic act of reducing the size of an organization's workforce, usually through a combination of layoffs, early retirement incentives, transfers, and natural attrition, and (2) the accompanying restructuring of surviving workers and work processes in response to the organization's altered size, resources, and goals. For the purposes of this book, whenever a downsized organization is mentioned, it is assumed that there are fewer workers than before and that reorganization or restructuring has taken place to redeploy the existing workforce.

Occasionally, a downsizing does not actually involve layoffs or other forms of attrition of personnel. It may simply involve a freeze on hiring, combined with increased production. Thus, "fewer workers" may mean fewer workers per unit of output. For example, an organization may expand into new markets. By doing so, it increases the amount of work generated and the size of the customer base that must be serviced with the existing number of workers. In effect, this scenario still meets both criteria of a reduced workforce and restructured organization. The organization has downsized, since fewer workers must now achieve higher units of output. It has restructured, since the existing workers must be redeployed and work processes and relationships altered. This allows the organization to manage inputs and outputs efficiently and to achieve renewed goals effectively.

Managers use a variety of terms, often euphemistically, to describe these twin activities of downsizing and restructuring. Below are just a dozen of the scores of labels and related strategies associated with downsizing and restructuring:

| | | |
|---|---|---|
| rightsizing | consolidating | reengineering |
| layoffs | demassifying | redeploying |
| streamlining | reduction-in-force (RIF) | reorganizing |
| retrenching | reshaping | reinventing |

I chose "downsizing" as a convenient way to refer to these activities, since it is the most widely recognized label to date. I do not, however, intend to oversimplify. There are some subtle and important differences among these concepts. For instance, reengineering is markedly different from most of the other strategies. It involves wiping the slate clean and literally starting the organization over from scratch. In reengineering the organization revises its mission and redesigns its business process and relationships to reduce costs and to improve efficiency, productivity, quality, and customer service. While survivors in the reengineered organizations I have worked with often endure the trauma of having to interview for their redesigned former jobs, reengineering may or may not involve layoffs.

Finally, I refer to downsizing as "strategic" because it is a deliberate choice made by an organization's leaders to create specific outcomes, such as reduced operating costs; improved efficiency, productivity, or competitiveness; and increased profits. Rather than a chance occurrence, such as mass attrition due to an organizational decline, downsizing is a business maneuver made either proactively, in anticipation of market demands, or reactively, in the face of actual threats to the organization's future.

When we think of the human toll of downsizing, we tend to spotlight those who lose their jobs. Eight years of consulting with downsizing organizations have led me to some sobering conclusions about those left to carry on. This book was inspired by these realizations:

- Survivors of downsizing often suffer as much as those who are laid off. In some ways they, like those laid off, are "victims." They suffer because they feel stuck in a codependent relationship with an organization they no longer trust.

- The managers of downsizing, like the employee survivors, also suffer. Their supposedly more privileged situation is compounded by several dilemmas, most notably how to be at once an ax-wielding warrior and a caring, trustworthy leader and how to promote organizational healing when they themselves are thrown off balance.

- Finally, the downsized organization suffers if survivors are not managed effectively. Healing organizations to be downsized takes careful prior planning for survivors' well-being. It cannot be an afterthought or be ignored, as is often the case.

There are many excellent business books on the market and many successful programs and processes for reengineering or reinventing organizations. Large corporations like IBM, AT&T, and General Motors have successfully downsized and restructured their organizations to be more lean and competitive. Yet, according to business analysts, many downsized organizations still fail to achieve their intended goals. This is linked to the challenge of revitalizing the remaining workforce. A 1992 survey of 1,200 human resources (HR) executives conducted by Right Associates, an international career management and HR consulting firm, showed that 72 percent of them found that their organization had not improved through its downsizing efforts. They also observed that 88 percent of the survivors of downsizing were given no training or assistance in how to function more effectively in the new environment. My own experiences as a management consultant is consistent with such observations. My client organizations who have downsized and restructured generally face a backlash from survivors, along with a host of previously unanticipated problems. We are beginning, however, to appreciate the lessons learned as organizations try to come to terms with the needs of survivors and survivor managers. David M. Noer, William Bridges, and others have contributed much to our understanding of what it takes to lead this kind of change in ways that revitalize the workers left to carry on.

This book is written from the perspective of the survivors: the managers and employees left to carry on in the aftermath of downsizing and restructuring. I do not intend, however, to diminish in any way the hardships and pain of those who lose their jobs to downsizing. My intent is to consider another effect of layoffs and to address the healing that must take place in business, government, education, health care, and other sectors as we respond to challenging economic and social realities.

To bring survivors' experiences to life for my readers, I interviewed scores of managers and employees in small and large and in public and private sector organizations in order to document their struggles and, most importantly, their successes. I offer their best practices so that we can all learn from the heroes and heroines who have found ways to make things work better.

# Chapter 1

—◊◊◊—

# THE DRAMA
# OF DOWNSIZING

John Vesta had mixed emotions when he landed in the position of general manager at Humex Corporation's Electronics Business Unit. He was relieved that the worst challenge of his lifetime career in marketing was behind him. He relished the prospect of transferring his executive and marketing skills to a new field of work within the industry he knew so well. It would be stimulating to experience organizational life from a totally different vantage point, as a general manager with several functions, in addition to sales, reporting to him. At the same time he had some concerns. He had taken a salary cut and a less senior position in an electronics company whose track record was spotty. And he was unclear about his charge "to help turn things around."

Before joining Humex, Vesta had been corporate vice president of sales and marketing at Zedco, a leading manufacturer of electronics and electrical equipment. Challenged by global heavy hitters in the Japanese and South Korean electronics industry, Zedco had begun to buckle under its own weight as it rapidly lost market share to these lower-priced competitors. Panic struck when the market share of the Microwave Devices Division plummeted from 40 percent to less than 5 percent, while the sales of fax machines dropped 50 percent over a twelve-month period.

Zedco's senior staff engaged the services of a large, reputable New York–based consulting firm to guide them through a strategic management process aimed at stemming the hemorrhaging loses and revitalizing the business. They adopted a seven-step planning process that involved (1) assessing marketplace threats and opportunities, (2) evaluating internal strengths and weaknesses, (3) reassessing Zedco's mission and direction, (4) formulating new goals and objectives, (5) identifying strategies to meet the new goals, (6) implementing the new strategies, and (7) follow-up and evaluation. After three months of intensive planning meetings, Zedco's senior management team made the fateful decision. Downsizing and restructuring would figure prominently in the new business strategy. They would get out of the microwave business, reduce the production and technical staff as well as management in the fax machines division, scale back on R&D activities, and look at several other cost-cutting measures. This would mean cutting nearly 30 percent of the jobs across the company.

Sales and marketing figured prominently. The decision to downsize and restructure strategically was based primarily on sales data and projections provided by John Vesta and his staff during the planning deliberations. The sales force and marketing staff, along with production, would obviously sustain the greatest cuts. This reduction-in-force translated into layoffs of 3,000 of Zedco's 11,000 employees. Over 2,000 of the eliminated jobs were in marketing, sales, and sales-related jobs such as field services and customer service. These jobs were all in Vesta's organization.

Vesta became a lead player in Zedco's downsizing. He lived daily with the agony of seeing the company, and especially his own staff, dwindle as employees and several peers with whom he had formed twenty-five–year friendships left the organization. His days became longer and harder to take. His nights were marked by interrupted fits of uneasy sleep. He sometimes lashed out at his family for no apparent reasons. He fell off his exercise routine and started smoking again after eight smoke-free years.

Vesta's work routine became a series of tense back-to-back meetings with senior management, human resources staff members, his own management staff, production managers, management consultants, the board of directors, divisional managers, and other affected groups. As one meeting rolled seamlessly into the next, he experienced the strain of totally losing control of his appointment book and his time. This stress was compounded by another: the endless dilemmas faced by all managers charged with downsizing.

For one thing, Vesta was forced to dismantle everything he had worked so hard to build over the previous eighteen years. In addition, he now lived daily with the paradox of emphasizing the company's manager-as-coach and team-player values, while asking his managers to wield an ax at the same time. He lived with feelings of incongruity and guilt from inflicting great pain in the lives of those asked to leave, yet needing to be a cheerleader for those who remained. How can I be at once a callous cost cutter and a trusted leader for surviving employees? he often wondered.

Vesta occasionally worried about his own fate. Perhaps the board members, the CEO, and the president—perhaps even his own peers—secretly blamed his staff's performance for Zedco's inability to compete. Perhaps they blamed him personally. Sure, they cited price competition as the official business reason. But what if they really believed that a high-performing sales and marketing team could have still generated sufficient business to beat the competition?

Vesta's close colleague, Sharon Smallman, manager of production at Zedco, harbored the same fears and faced the same dilemmas as she led the elimination of 930 production jobs. She too dealt with the "be-a-coach-but-wield-an-ax" paradox. She too felt the irony of trying to be a judicious cost cutter while remaining in the good graces of her surviving employees. She struggled to maintain her morale and her employees' motivation in the face of it all. At times she felt resentful toward senior management, including her boss, the vice president of production, and even her trusted collaborator, John

Vesta, with whom she had worked closely for eight years on shared production and marketing concerns. She often thought, They get support and praise from the stockholders for their bold, decisive stance to save the company, while we middle- and first-line managers have to do the actual firings and bear the brunt of employee resentment.

In fact, in many ways Smallman felt like her own employees. Like them she felt resentful, stressed, ambivalent, and insecure about her future with the company. Yet at times she also envied her employees as they banded together, venting, grieving, and forming a sort of victims' support group for one another. Because she was part of the problem, she certainly couldn't expect compassion from her harried, skeptical employees. Inclusion in their support network was not an option. Her peers in middle- and frontline management were too busy handling layoffs and their aftershocks to support themselves, let alone one another. As a manager she felt isolated.

At the same time she was plagued by guilt about having such feelings. She knew the business reasons for the decision to downsize as well as anyone. She had seen it coming. In fact, in her heart she knew that if she had been a member of the senior staff she would have made the same decision. Her pain was compounded by the lack of emotional support she received as a middle manager. Only once in all the business journals she subscribed to had she read any material directed at the manager's plight in all of this. It was in a 1994 *Fortune* magazine article, "Burned-Out Bosses," that author Lee Smith wrote, "Nothing—not overwork, not confusion, not lost perks, not apprehension—is as deadening to a manager's morale as firing subordinates."

But her colleague John Vesta seemed to roll with the punches very well. Smallman thought about a conversation she had had two years earlier with Vesta and Burt Barnes, Zedco's head of total quality management. Vesta, Barnes, and Smallman were close collaborators during the implementation of Zedco's TQM process. Barnes, in a moment of uncertainty, had confided his doubts about whether quality could really sustain the company's competitive edge in the face of more competitive prices from Asian counterparts. Smallman was not surprised when Vesta responded to Barnes's musings with a pep talk about "creating need in customers by assuring value." In fact, she had come to admire Vesta's candor, his visionary outlook, and his belief in his ability to make things happen.

Smallman decided to put her reservations aside and seek out Vesta to see how he was handling the current situation. Perhaps she could gain some encouragement from his typically positive outlook. Perhaps he could tell her something that would put things in a different perspective. After playing telephone tag for five days, they were able to speak and to eke out a forty-five–minute breakfast meeting at 6:30 A.M. three weeks later. (Vesta's secretary was unable to assist in setting up the meeting since she was now supporting several other staff members as well as Vesta and since Vesta, in an attempt to control his time, had decided to manage his own appointments.)

"I just wanted to touch base with you and see how things are going for you with our restructuring process," Sharon began as they sat down to breakfast.

"Ah, cut the business-speak, Sharon," Vesta interrupted in his usual candid style. "We know each other too well to be oblique. You've got bags under your eyes, and you're looking pretty beat up, just like me!"

"Well, thanks for the pep talk. That's just what I came for." They laughed uneasily, then relaxed into the moment. "You know, sometimes I feel like we're making this up as we go along," Smallman continued. She paused, waiting for Vesta's reaction.

"Well, it's not like we've ever been down this path before. Although by now there's plenty of precedents in other companies. We might benefit from benchmarking their best practices."

"Now who's using business-speak?" Smallman teased. "You know companies aren't anxious to come forward and brag about their successes with downsizing. The verdict's still out in most cases, I think. They may be cutting costs, but are they really more profitable? Are they really achieving their business goals? I'm not sure. Besides, the minute they go on the record as being a 'success story,' some unforeseen challenge comes up and there they go—out of business or at best downsizing again."

"Am I detecting cynicism from you, Sharon? That's really out of character for you—the champion of total quality management, the one who spearheaded Zedco's march into the cellular phone business . . ."

"Okay, John, I hear one of your motivational speeches coming on. I usually find them inspiring, but not today. Look, this downsizing business is serious. It's not something I bargained for in my career. I hope I never have to go through this again."

"Me neither," the vice president of sales acknowledged.

Two months later, on the completion of Zedco's reorganization, John Vesta was summoned to a luncheon meeting with the CEO, Jim Furley, at the lavish Executives' Club in town. As he drove to the meeting, his thoughts turned to a particularly tense planning session a month earlier, at which a division manager had challenged the company's "reckless, sweeping changes." Furley's response was to quickly dismiss the manager's protests, admonishing him, "Leadership is not for the faint of heart. If dealing with transformational change is too much for you, you might want to consider another line of work."

Furley was new to the company. In an unprecedented move in Zedco's forty-year history the company had recruited the CEO from a totally different industry. The board of directors had determined that a "fresh perspective" was needed. Furley was legendary for his ability to take unprecedented risks and make sweeping, innovative changes. For example, in his previous position as president of an office products manufacturing firm, he had led his company into a joint venture with a competitor in order to develop a new line of high-tech, ergonomically correct recliners that provided massages and nature sounds music, among other features. The competitor had the technology that Furley's company lacked to create the line. Furley had the capital they needed. Together, the companies were able to drive one of the larger players out of the market. Zedco's stock had risen when news of Furley's arrival hit the street. But in spite of his great credentials, Furley failed to impress Vesta. They had had an uneasy relationship from the start.

"This is difficult for me," Furley began, "so let me just get straight to the point. I'm going to have to ask for your resignation. You and I have had some differences, but this has nothing to do with that. In light of our new strategic direction, I will be making some changes in the position you currently hold." The rest of the conversation whirled by in the stream of thoughts and questions spinning in Vesta's head. He felt confused, betrayed. Surely Furley knew all along my job was on the cutting block. Why didn't he warn me? Oh, he wanted to make sure that I wasn't demoralized as I led my outfit's downsizing. Why is he calling it a "resignation"? What a jerk. What do I do now? What do I say? Vesta came back to reality when Furley started to outline the terms of his severance package. "Of course, as a faithful, long-standing member of this company's management team, the terms of your separation will be quite lucrative." He was given a very generous golden parachute and thought he had landed on his feet five months later as the new general manager of Humex Corporation's Electronics Business Unit.

Vesta's new position required that he spend six months at Humex's corporate headquarters and in the field learning the business. He would then permanently move to the Cincinnati-based business unit to "effect a turnaround" of the small organization of 320 employees.

Vesta was excited about his new position at Humex. His termination from Zedco had occurred just three weeks after his eldest daughter, one of five children, had left for college. He was pleasantly surprised to have found a stimulating new position so soon. Many of his laid-off colleagues hadn't fared as well. He looked forward to the challenge of transferring his years of big business expertise to revitalizing a small operation. "It will be more like a hobby," he told his wife, "less stress and a chance to get quick, tangible results, even if it means a pay cut."

In his enthusiasm, Vesta had asked very few questions of his interviewers at Humex. It was enough to know that he would report directly to the president. It was enough to know that he would have a great deal of decision-making autonomy. He was encouraged by the prospects for advancement and excited about the opportunity to lead a turnaround.

Six months after starting his position, the president called Vesta into his office for a final briefing before his transfer from corporate headquarters to the new business unit office. Reality came crashing down around him. The "turnaround" was really a "turnover," another euphemism for a sweeping downsizing of the workforce. The grand corporate design, the nuances of which Vesta had given little attention to, added up to the following reality: his business unit staff was to be reduced from 320 to fewer than 200 employees under his leadership.

Of four departments in the division, three departments would survive. Of fourteen managers, nine would remain. Thirty field service representatives would be eliminated. Thirty-five technical specialists were to be cut. Approximately seventy other miscellaneous positions across the board had to be eliminated. Headquarters would need Vesta's input after he got the lay of the land to determine which ones specifically to cut.

Vesta was stunned and disappointed by his naiveté. How could he have missed the writing on the wall? Of course Humex wanted him. He had successfully executed a major downsizing at his former company. He had chosen to work for a relatively small company, hoping that he would not have to endure the challenges of downsizing again. And here he was, a little over a year later, facing the same scenario.

The employees at Humex waited with trepidation, fueled by rampant rumors, for the arrival of the new general manager. The cafeteria conversation typically went like this:

We heard he's a hatchet man from Zedco. He laid off over 10,000 employees there.

Come on, it couldn't be that many; Zedco only had 11,000 employees. I know because they used to be one of our main competitors before they shifted their focus to the cellular phone business.

Well maybe it was 1,000 people that he laid off. But that's still bad. He's still Jack the Knife. The minute they transferred the last general manager, I knew we were in trouble. She was tough, but fair. She was concerned about her people. They wanted to get someone more ruthless in here.

I heard they're planning to eliminate the entire marketing department and centralize everything at corporate.

That can't be true. That would never work.

Well they just did something similar at my wife's company, and she works in a business unit about the same size as this one.

I'm really losing my motivation. You just never know what management's going to do to us next. They're running around in stretch limousines and corporate jets at headquarters cooking up all kinds of changes without having a clue about what we do down here.

On arriving at the business unit, Vesta was greeted with polite ambivalence. The acting general manager escorted him to his new office, went over a few important transition details in the morning, took him to lunch at an elaborate local restaurant, along with his new administrative assistant so that they could get acquainted informally, offered some polite good luck sentiments, and then left him to run the show. Vesta spent the rest of the afternoon walking around to visit members of his new management staff individually on their turf. (He had read in a management textbook somewhere that this was a nice interpersonal touch, especially when entering a new or a somewhat hostile environment to take charge.) He took the opportunity to remind each of them personally that he had called an all-day management staff meeting for that coming Friday to review goals and expectations and to solicit their input and concerns.

At the Friday staff meeting his management team was attentive, if somewhat aloof. They dispassionately took notes and asked benign questions about his "vision for the business unit," his "strategic intent," his "leadership style and expectations" of them, and so forth. The slight hint of tension in the conference room shifted into full-blown antagonism when Yvonne Wright, who had been nervously fidgeting in her seat all day, suddenly asked, "Is it true what they're saying—have you been sent here to lead a massive reduction-in-force? I need to know if our jobs are on the chopping block."

Vesta felt the blood rush to his face as he looked her in the eye, responding coolly in a staccato voice, "At the present time, we have made no major commitments to change of any kind. I have yet to get the lay of the land, look at performance, size things up. So, to repeat, I have no immediate intentions of making any sweeping modifications to the way you've been doing business around here."

It was with apprehension that the man who had earlier in his career earned a positive reputation for his candor and his honesty eyed the woman who had demonstrated the guts to ask what was on everyone's mind. He knew from her expression that his nonanswer was transparent and unacceptable. He also knew that she had enough business savvy not to force the issue. As the meeting adjourned, he regretted his double-talk. He worried that his integrity and trustworthiness were shot and his leadership credibility irreparably damaged. Honor and truthfulness were high on his list of personal values. (He had reaffirmed this at a three-day seminar led by management consultants at his former job.) Now the members of his new staff would soon find out that, in effect, he had lied. But how could he have answered in the affirmative? Five of the managers present would be among those laid off, but first he had to lead them through reductions of their own staff. To reveal the corporate plans at this point would be premature. At the same time his anxiety escalated as he faced the realization that his double-talk had raised other questions which the managers' growing trepidation and skepticism would prevent them from asking. He recalled the betrayal and anger he felt when, in his former job, Zedco's CEO and his immediate superior, the president, had failed to warn him that his own position would eventually be eliminated. Way to go! he thought, admonishing himself sarcastically. Great way to earn the trust of your new staff.

In the weeks that followed, the management staff and the rest of the business unit employees viewed Vesta's frequent flights to corporate headquarters with growing suspicion. "Something's up," they kept saying to one another. They were right. On his corporate visits Vesta experienced déjà vu as he relived the endless planning meetings in preparation for Humex's reduction-in-force. He met with senior management to identify those who would be affected: people in sales, customer service, field service, and technical support, as well as human resources staff members. Together they established criteria: performance in sales, individual performance ratings, length of service, Equal Employment Opportunity Commission (EEOC) regulations to prevent class-action suits by people in certain age, racial, or gender groups. They even examined how much each job cost the company and therefore what the savings would be if the job were eliminated. For legal reasons, however, this last criterion was never put in writing. They then prepared written guidelines for business unit managers to use to direct their decision making.

Then came the final stages of the planning process: communicating the event to the business unit HR staff and to the immediate supervisors of those affected, along with the designated date for the layoffs. The guidelines for carrying out the layoffs included the following:

> Take no more than six minutes to execute the discussion. . . .
> Be sure that the decision is the first thing you mention: "Based on business reasons, heavy competition, your position has been eliminated."

Finally the guidelines for discussing severance terms were given:

> Based on your length of service you are eligible for a severance package that includes two weeks of salary for each year served, and two weeks in lieu of service since you must leave right away, continuation of health and other benefits for two months from your date of separation. Human Resources will be in touch with you to work out other details connected with your 401(k) plan and other matters.

The downsizing went without a hitch. The affected employees entered the designated offices, received their orders, met with HR, cleared out their desks, and left the same day. Their stunned, surviving former colleagues wandered the hallways from task to task like the dazed walking wounded, waiting for the next bombshell to hit.

The rumor mill processed each firing with unrelenting fury, grinding out story after story about the events at the business unit:

> Did you know that Jennifer Laskey had just gotten news that they're expecting a child and they had just closed on a new house that requires two salaries to pay the mortgage?

> I heard that the guys down in data processing are planning to file a class-action suit.

> That will be useless because I have it from a good source that they're going to close down the entire operation within a year.

> Do you think that's why they've brought in all those management consultants?

> They seem to have money to spend on stuff like that—stuff that they think is more important than our jobs.

> Well, did you see the CEO from corporate when he was here yesterday? He arrived from the airport in a stretch limousine. What's up with those guys? They could save two full-time jobs for the price of the trip out here.

You know what my supervisor said to us yesterday? He said, "You're going to have to produce twice as much as before to meet our business projections, or we'll all be out of a job!"

Yeah, so now it's our fault if the place goes under.

Vesta was now even more stressed than during the Zedco layoffs. This was partly because two bouts with layoffs were too much to take but also because in a small organization he was much closer to, less insulated from, the action. His proximity to those who had left and those who remained enabled him to get more direct feedback. He learned that, while the surviving managers on his immediate staff were disappointed in his role, they basically liked him as a person. Some secretly hoped that he could eventually renew what was left of the organization.

Following his experience at the first staff meeting, he had openly revealed his discomfort with not having been able to give full information at that point, and he had given his staff assurances that he would never again keep them in the dark about important business decisions. He was able to regain an uneasy trust with his senior management team. But, as they moved forward, they waited for more consistent demonstrations that Vesta would keep his word about including them in the communications loop. The surviving employees, including line supervisors and those reporting directly to them, however, did not by any means come to trust their new general manager.

Vesta engaged my consulting firm to guide him through the process of rebuilding his shell-shocked organization. In addition to providing useful expertise and a fresh external perspective, we became a sounding board for Vesta—a place where he and his management team could vent frustrations, strategize, and talk through their own losses and concerns as they led the necessary changes. A good bit of the dialogue also focused on "managing self to lead others." I shared with Vesta the *Fortune* magazine article "Burned-Out Bosses," which deals with the stresses and challenges of survivor managers. Inspired by the article, he began to pay closer attention to his own needs in order to be more effective at leading others. He started exercising and gave up smoking again. He resolved to leave the tensions of the workplace behind at the end of each day and to move through this challenge systematically and with courage.

We advised Vesta to begin to focus on the survivors: the managers and employees left to carry on the business. We suggested that he needed to get honest feedback from his employees about their perceptions, feelings, and stance toward the organization, as well as input about how to make things better. To gather this information, we scheduled a series of focus group interviews with all employees.

Our first focus group meeting was held off-site in a quiet conference room. We had gotten word that employees were upset about having to take time off from an already overburdened schedule to talk about their reactions. Skeptical about management's intentions, they had expressed their view that time and money would be better spent rehiring their laid-off colleagues. When we arrived, the anger in the conference room was palpable. My colleague and I were expecting fourteen participants. Six came at the expected hour. Three others trickled in reluctantly during the first hour of our two-hour meeting. We wearily eyed the wall clock, earnestly trying to satisfy our client, John Vesta, but beginning to feel the strain of the unrelenting negative energy directed at us.

I led the interview, encouraging employees to offer their "candid feedback to senior management" concerning the impact of the company's latest RIF. My associate captured comments verbatim with her laptop computer:

> *Employee 1:* You want me to "tell the truth as I see it"? Well, okay. I resent all this talk about "empowerment" and "ownership" of the business and us being "number one."

> *Employee 2:* Yeah. We don't "own" this business. We don't have any power. Nobody really cares what we think; they just want to make the numbers. We don't need this. What we need is honest leaders who know what the hell they're doing. Why do they always lie to us?

*Employee 3:* I resent what this company is doing to us. And I resent this meeting. This is a sham. They're not going to change anything.

The question forming in my mind felt like a pathetic cliché: "How do the rest of you feel about what John, Ricardo, and Gloria just said?"

*Employees:* (In unison) We agree!

This was immediately followed by a flurry of side conversations as participants compared notes and shared specific examples of their experiences and the morale issues related to having to "do more with less." I invited them to refocus, reminding them that the goal of the session was to generate and prioritize specific recommendations to management about ways to better support employee efforts "now that the downsizing process is over."

*Employee 4:* That's another lie. It's not over. We heard that they plan to close down this entire unit eventually.

*Employee 5:* Yeah. I don't believe a thing they say. We're just a variable cost to be cut—not real people. They don't care anymore. Twenty-five years ago, when I started with this company, it was a different place.

These so-called survivors of a downsized organization were expressing predictable sentiments. They went on, over the next hour and a half, to explain their frustrations and their reactions. They felt like the survivors of downsizing I meet in every sector in which I consult:

- *insecure, skeptical, or hopeless* about their future and the organization's future;
- *mistrustful* of management—"Do they have our best interests at heart?" "Do they know what they're doing?" "Are they telling the truth?"

- *stressed and burned out* by increased responsibilities and less support;
- *ambivalent or guilty* about their survivor status—"I'm glad it wasn't me, but sometimes I wonder why not me. Some of my colleagues who were let go had more seniority and more talent than I do."
- *betrayed* by managers who in some cases said "don't worry" one day and implemented layoffs the next;
- *angry and grief stricken* about the losses;
- *disillusioned* by the apparent inconsistencies between actions taken and the company rhetoric—"empowerment," "teamwork," "employee-centered organization," and "people are our first priority," as well as the use of euphemisms like "decruitment" and "rightsizing";
- *demotivated* and ready to adopt the attitude that "it's just a job";
- *vulnerable and unappreciated* by a company that they felt would readily lay them off, like their peers before them, if necessary.

Vesta read the consultants' report from the focus groups with great interest. On reading the first few pages he concluded that the employees' comments and their anger and fear revealed a lack of understanding of the business reasons that had driven the decision. He thought that he had done a good job of communicating this, but obviously his message had not been heard. According to this report the employees felt that the business unit managers, like corporate management, had been ill-advised in their decision making. Most employees insisted that the business reasons given were not legitimate ones and that the organization was now less viable than before the changes.

As he read on, Vesta became increasingly alarmed. His employees claimed that those who were involuntarily separated from the organization were treated unfairly and that their lives had been disrupted unnecessarily. Some speculated that in time the company would have to turn around and rehire the employees who were let go or, worse, hire new ones to replace them. Others speculated that contract workers would replace laid-off workers, creating chaos and further damaging morale. Still others maintained that the company would eventually fail because of the decision to downsize and restructure. Most of all, Humex's survivors felt that they were themselves treated even more unfairly than those who left. They were, they believed, expected to work harder with fewer resources and no compassion from management. The consultants' report also mentioned a term Vesta had never encountered before: "high turnover intent." This meant that most employees were looking to leave the company if they could find another job.

Vesta's resolve was badly shaken by the consultants' reports from the focus groups. He clearly had underestimated the emotional toll levied by this act of downsizing. He became painfully aware of his lack of skill and sensitivity in dealing with employees and promoting healing in the aftermath of downsizing. It occurred to him that the employees themselves needed to develop coping strategies to size up their situation, rebuild their morale, advance their needs, and find ways to make their fullest contributions through work. Without these skills, his organization ran the risk of further experiencing the very symptoms it had set out to alleviate by downsizing: sluggish productivity, high costs, and diminished profits.

Unfortunately, John Vesta's story is too often true for downsizing organizations everywhere. The typical organization gives more thought to easing the transition for those who are removed from the workforce than for those who remain behind. Survivors are expected to pick up the slack and outperform the competition as though it were business as usual. While some laid-off employees receive early retirement options, severance packages, career counseling, outplacement services, and golden parachutes to ease the pain of separation, those left behind must tend their own wounds and forge bravely ahead. But they do not. Instead, this ailing group experiences what some management experts now call "survivor syndrome." Their morale level is at an all-time low. They adopt an "us"-versus-"them" mentality toward management. They develop a culture of blaming, rather than collaboration, in which each level blames the next higher level. They become fearful of risk taking and as a result are less creative. And their extreme stress levels, as they do more with less, ultimately result in diminished productivity.

# Chapter 2

—◊—

# THE SURVIVOR'S CHALLENGE: HEALING THE WOUNDS OF A BROKEN PACT

She had been quiet throughout my entire focus group meeting. Unassuming, somewhat distracted, seemingly disinterested, she scribbled a few notes from time to time. At the end of the session, after everyone had left, she hung around to talk to me. "I wanted to give you this," she said, offering me a doodle-filled page from her yellow notepad. "I wasn't sure whether it was appropriate, but I decided to share it with you anyway."

In a burst of creativity fueled by pain, she had scrawled a poem arranged in the shape of a pyramid:

*On*
*the mean side*
*of "leaner and meaner"*
*we huddle fearfully waiting for the next cut,*
*dreading the next blow to fragile psyches worn thin*
*by broken promises. Trust betrayed. Love of work lost.*
*Hopes for a secure future dashed against the hard cold reality*
*of mergers, acquisitions, cutbacks, and layoffs.*

I was impressed. "This is good! Where did you find it?"

"Oh, I just wrote it as I sat here listening to everyone moan and groan about the changes. You know, it made me realize one thing. It made me realize how lucky I am to have a husband in an excellent, secure job."

Ten months later, in December, I received one of those extremely personal holiday letters chronicling her family's life events over the previous year. "Jim lost his job last summer," the letter read. "We are now in Vermont where he took a lesser position with a major salary cut. I have decided to stay at home with the boys for a while . . . a very different lifestyle . . . a lot less money to spend . . . taking time to reflect, reassess . . . the cats are doing well. . . ."

## THE PSYCHOLOGICAL TOLL OF DOWNSIZING

Everyone suffers initially after downsizing and restructuring. This is normal. The layoff victims lose their income and position and must endure the pressure of rebuilding their livelihood and their emotional well-being. The survivors feel the shock of the loss of their colleagues, their certainty, their feeling of competence, and their job identity. They worry about their importance to the organization in the future. The pain for survivor managers is intensified by the fact that they are held responsible for everyone's suffering. A Westinghouse survivor manager reminded me recently that he lies awake at night worrying not just about himself and his own family's future but about his subordinates and their families as well. Finally, the organization as a whole suffers, having had to amputate parts of itself in order to survive. In some cases the organization's trauma is compounded by the realization that the layoffs were ill-advised or did not bring the expected gains in stability, productivity, or profits.

The managerial use of the term "survivor" in this context is an ironic but sadly appropriate one. It acknowledges that a type of carnage is taking place in organizations today. It implies that there are two camps: one for casualties who leave the organization, and the other for the more fortunate survivors who remain. This awareness is taking a steady toll on the psyche of the American workforce. In 1990 only 20 percent of American employees surveyed by the International Survey Research Corporation were concerned about being laid off.

Six years later, 64 percent reported being fearful of losing their job. A 1992 survey of 1,200 human resources executives conducted by Right Associates showed 70 percent noting that, following downsizing, employees lacked confidence in their ability to negotiate a successful career. Seventy-two percent also reported that the employees they counseled felt the organization had not improved through its downsizing efforts. In many cases there were little time and few resources for assisting employees in coping with their perceived and real losses. The same Right Associates survey showed, for example, that 88 percent of the employees who survived downsizing were given no training or assistance in how to function more effectively in the new environment.

The emotional price of downsizing has become the subject of weekly articles in newspapers and business journals in the nineties. A November 1995 *Academy of Management Executive* article, "Voices of Survivors: Words That Downsizing CEOs Should Hear," offers this assessment:

> The real pains of downsizing cannot be minimized. Careers change, families struggle, and downsized victims suffer loss of prestige, income and security. While a few downsized individuals may be victims of their own past inefficiency, the vast number are those who have performed well and played by the rules. . . . The irony of this situation is that the individual and social costs of downsizing can only be justified if the effort leads to a healthier organization. Yet much evidence suggests that organizations do not substantively improve after downsizing.

A January 1996 *Personnel Journal* article, "Teach Downsizing Survivors How to Thrive," offers this prognosis:

> Now, there's not only no career growth to look forward to, there's no immediate job security either. . . . Though job losses

may have slowed in the private sector, they're accelerating in the public sector. . . . The biggest threat to service workers may not be corporate greed, but the advent of technology. . . . At risk are a wide array of occupations, including mortgage brokers, ticket agents, sales clerks, typists and delivery people.

As their organizations make sweeping changes, survivors who referred to themselves as "IBMers" or "Alcoans" now face the pain of disidentification with whatever that label meant in the past. Out of this loss of identity and trepidation about the future comes low morale, a kind of suffering that attacks the vitality or the spirit of the workforce. "I used to love to come to work," they say, but "now it's just a job." The attempt to disengage from an intimate relationship with the organization is, some might argue, a healthy attempt to protect the psyche during the pain of loss. By putting emotional distance between themselves and the now estranged entity for which they work, the survivor hopes to minimize the damage to his or her own soul.

In my leadership seminars I ask participants to indicate by a show of hands whether they find their work joyous, fulfilling, and meaningful. With each year that passes, the number of affirmative responses diminishes. The only exception is in the not-for-profit sector (where, by the way, salaries are lower and job security virtually nonexistent!). When I explore why not-for-profit executives and service providers still find their work meaningful, even in hard times brought on by funding cutbacks, they tell me two things: because they chose to do their line of work not for the money but for the chance to "make a difference in people's lives," and because of the personal and spiritual growth they experience as a result.

Thus, healing the downsized organization has much to do with healing the soul of the worker. Survivors who find that the organization's vision and direction may no longer be compatible with their own beliefs, hopes, and dreams about the future are in a quandary. They may work their way out of this predicament by creating alternate options for themselves, within or outside the organization. Or they may recommit themselves to the organization, working to promote its healing and renewal and embracing its dreams as their own. It is in the individual's best interest to do the former. It is in the organization's best interests to encourage the latter. True organizational healing requires a combination of both attitudes.

In his book *Healing the Wounds: Overcoming the Trauma of Layoffs and Revitalizing Downsized Organizations,* David M. Noer reminds us that "the battle to ward off and eventually develop an immunity to these survivor symptoms must be waged simultaneously by individuals and organizations." Unfortunately, most survivors have neither the expertise, resources, nor energy to wage this battle. They are caught, rather, in the struggle to make sense of an increasingly perilous work world.

Like the people who were the subject of the survivor's poem at the start of this chapter, John Vesta's employees believed that they were living "on the mean side of 'leaner and meaner.'" They experienced the changes as a win-lose situation in which they bore the brunt of the losses. They viewed their laid-off colleagues as casualties and themselves as the walking wounded. Vesta, along with his management team, had become the enemy.

Employees in both camps, the survivors felt, had been wronged by an organization that lured them in with the promise of career possibilities and a reliable livelihood. They reacted not like lucky survivors but like wounded victims left to heal themselves without sufficient time or resources to do so. The security, trust, loyalty, and unquestioning commitment of the organization man of the fifties were replaced for this new breed of nineties workers by the feelings they expressed in Humex Corporation's focus groups:

- survivor shock and denial;
- grief and anger;
- ambivalence and survivor guilt;
- fear and distrust;
- disillusionment and demotivation;

- feeling unappreciated or undervalued;
- excessive stress from work overload and the impact of the above feelings.

These are the symptoms of survivor syndrome. Let's examine each more closely to understand the phenomenon and its impact on the individual as well as the organizational psyche.

## Survivor Shock and Denial

The most critical step in the healing process is facing the reality of the situation at hand. Yet this is also the most difficult step to take. Human nature dictates that, faced with the shock of an affront to our security, we first turn to denial. In this state of disbelief, we find a momentary, and necessary, safe harbor. Our denial inoculates us against the dis-ease of our losses, giving us a chance to maintain our bearing and perhaps maintain our sanity. Our denial holds the promise that perhaps things will return to normal, perhaps the situation in which we find ourselves is a temporary aberration that will right itself under the pressure of our protest.

Such is the case with today's employees and their employers, faced with the challenge of a dramatically changed workplace in which old promises and cherished premises no longer hold true. This point came home for me rather profoundly when I worked as a stress management counselor for Volkswagen during the closing of their Westmoreland, Pennsylvania, plant in 1987. To the very end many of the workers I counseled remained stuck in this phase of denial, holding on to the fantasy that "Ford is coming to acquire us," even as the last doors of the plant were closed. So profound was the shock for some of the workers who believed in job security that, even when faced with the certainty of their "decruitment," they secretly believed that "it can't be happening to us."

While shock and denial are natural first reactions to loss, as the popular literature on death and dying teaches us, to heal ourselves we must find ways to move through subsequent stages of anger, bargaining, depression, and finally acceptance. But this is easier said than done, particularly in situations where there is no permission given to acknowledge the loss and move through the grieving process toward recovery.

## Grief and Anger

Survivors who have moved through their shock and denial experience different degrees of grief and anger. Grief is anguish and distress caused by loss or other pain inflicted on our lives. Anger is the indignation we feel about the loss that causes our grief. Anger may be turned inward, resulting in depression, or directed at others in various forms of retaliation.

When Sharon Smallman, the production manager at Zedco lost her colleague John Vesta to the corporate ax, she let go of her last vestiges of denial to face her full-blown anger. She was enraged. Not only had she lost a close friend and professional confidant, but she also felt angry about the way things had been handled. She had endured the layoffs as well as could be expected, but John's leaving made her feel personally vulnerable as a member of the management team. In her mind fairness had not prevailed. Embittered, she entertained the idea of resigning in protest, but she quickly came to her senses as she recalled her car note and mortgage. So, she "quit and stayed." She became one of those employees who mutter under their breath that "it's just a job." Work lost its potency in her life. She went from being an exemplary, high-performing, almost overzealous manager to being one who no longer put in extra hours to wrestle with new ideas or mentor young professionals. She adopted a personal rule of no more weekend hours, no more working past five o'clock. She no longer looked forward to her daily routine of going to the office early to share a special coffee hour with her favorite colleagues. Driven by her grief and anger, she began to do the minimum to get by and keep her job.

## Ambivalence and Survivor Guilt

I recently counseled an employee who was experiencing survivor guilt about her status after her company's massive layoffs. "I sometimes wonder whether I was spared because I'm the only female technician in my work unit," Marva confided. "Some of my colleagues who were let go were more seasoned than I am." Marva had sought advice during one of my leadership seminars, one in which she was the only woman in a group of twenty-six employees. She carried these feelings in spite of the fact that her particular job was critical to the survival of her operation and in spite of the fact that in her performance reviews she consistently had "exceeded expectations." Her perception had framed her experience so that it evoked guilt and self-doubt. Her performance was beginning to suffer as she lost sleep worrying about whether her shortcomings would be discovered and whether her colleagues saw her as a benefactor of affirmative action. She was becoming increasingly tense and distracted at work—all as a result of her preoccupation with guilt feelings.

One way our subconscious mind seeks to resolve guilt feelings is to attract its own punishment. When Marva chose to think and feel that she should have been the one laid off, since her colleagues who were let go were more competent, she unwittingly set herself up to make choices that confirmed her belief, thereby evoking the antidote for guilt: punishment. Mired in her guilt, she became less productive and less creative. In the jargon of psychology, she experienced a "self-fulfilling prophecy."

Of course, there are healthier ways to resolve guilt feelings. We may choose not to give them credence in the first place, reminding ourselves that guilt is justified only when we have actually done harm to someone. We may examine all the facts in the situation to maintain objectivity in assessing our role and determining a more appropriate response. Or we may take measures to affirm our self-worth and seek to create viable career alternatives for ourselves. We will address such options later.

*Fear and Distrust*

Loss of trust in management is the most predictable symptom of survivor syndrome. Trust is the willingness to be vulnerable to another based on a belief that the other is competent and benevolent and will act with integrity toward the truster. That is rarely, if ever, the case with survivors in a downsizing environment.

When corporations choose to reduce the size of their workforce, those who remain ask three questions related to (1) competence—"Do they know what they're doing?" (2) benevolence—"Do they care about its impact on us? Do they have our best interests at heart?" and (3) integrity—"Are they acting in a consistently honest, principled way? Are they telling us the truth?" To establish and maintain trust, managers must make choices that allow survivors to answer yes to these questions. Unfortunately, managers can't always do this. Multiple ways of downsizing, often following the promise of no more layoffs, violate the question of competence. Eliminating jobs, and therefore people, as costs to be cut brings into question the issue of benevolence. And the almost inevitable dearth of communication and consistent messages flies in the face of integrity, at least from the survivors' viewpoint.

Thus, fear and distrust become predictable survivor responses. The fear is rooted in a concern about whether the organization's leaders really know what they are doing and whether they can continue to satisfy the workers' need for security. The distrust is a natural outgrowth of the fear. It reflects a lack of confidence that managers have the wherewithal to ensure the outcomes they desire for shareholders, customers, and employees and the courage to tell the truth about their capabilities.

Survivor fear and distrust are also brought on by the very nature of the conditions surrounding downsizing. Survivors observe that good employees and good managers are among the casualties. They notice that whole departments can be core to the business one year and excessed the next. Struck by the ap-

parent randomness of job eliminations and layoffs in his organization, a survivor in one of my focus groups, waiting for the
next round of firings, described them as "corporate drive-by
shootings." Another spoke of "being held hostage by an organization that is likely to execute me at any moment regardless of
my actions." While not all survivors use such strong metaphors
to depict their fear and distrust of the situation in which they
find themselves, it is safe to say that most experience this loss of
equilibrium as a frightening work and life event.

The comments of the survivors in the focus group cited in
chapter 1 capture the apprehension and loss felt by survivors of
downsizing in every sector in which I have worked:

> This is a sham. They're not going to change anything.

> That's another lie. It's not over.

> I don't believe a thing they say. We're just a variable cost to be
> cut—not real people. They don't care anymore. Twenty-five
> years ago . . . it was a different place.

These comments carry the seeds of distrust, as defined
above:

- "They don't have our best interests at heart."
- "They don't know what they're doing."
- "They're not telling us the whole truth."

Real or imagined, these are the beliefs that, in my opinion,
have caused trust to emerge as the most pressing leadership issue of the nineties.


## Disillusionment and Demotivation

As is human nature, survivors act in ways that are consistent
with, or that confirm, their beliefs. Because they doubt that
managers are benevolent—caring about their best interests—
they become disillusioned. As a result, survivors may take

fewer, if any, risks. For the same reason, and also because they fear repercussions, they may withhold ideas and information. In a climate in which the stakes are high, it is easy to conclude that one must exercise caution and hold on to information for its pale promise of power. Because they have lost faith in managerial competence, survivors may question the legitimacy of the business decisions surrounding downsizing and restructuring. Disillusioned employees at all levels find it easy to engage in a cycle of blame, in which each layer blames the one above it for the insecurity and job overload and for the other feelings and experiences associated with working in a downsizing, restructuring organization. Because they doubt that management is acting with integrity, survivors become skeptical of whatever they are told. Second-guessing their own and management's decisions becomes a way of life. Motivation wanes in the face of all of this, and inevitably the employees' best talents are withheld.

In one large manufacturing company for which my firm provides leadership training, technical professionals and managers alike consistently challenge our teaching of the importance of risk taking if they are to innovate and indeed heal their downsizing company. They cite their fears about imagined repercussions for trying something new or for telling the truth as they see it, another of our teachings that initially gets rejected. In effect, by suppressing their imagination and information, they mimic the very behavior they criticize in senior management.

## Feeling Unappreciated or Undervalued

Scott O'Grady's exaltation to hero status was indeed an unusual occurrence, for in our culture true heroes tend to be the martyred or the rescuers of victims. Scott O'Grady, however, was a survivor. A U.S. pilot shot down by Bosnian Serbs on June 2, 1995, his F-16 cut in two, low on food and surrounded by hostile forces, he survived for nearly a week, bolstered by prayer and a diet of insects. In a truly heroic act, a group of Marine pilots finally rescued O'Grady. But they were not acclaimed the heroes; O'Grady was. He returned home to a cheering, adoring crowd as schoolchildren sang the national anthem on his behalf. His face sold newspapers and magazines—perhaps eventually books. The president of the United States invited him to lunch. Americans praised his integrity— he was a genuinely nice guy, deeply spiritual, hardworking, committed, resourceful, inspiring. They wondered out loud if Tom Cruise would play him in the movie.

"Why the fuss?" one of my friends quipped when the news first hit the headlines in early June. "He didn't do anything— he just saved his own ass!" This may have been a rather crude depiction of a celebrated event, but nonetheless it was a sentiment shared by many. Some people wrote scathing editorials to protest what they saw as a debasement of heroism. "He's not a hero; he's just a survivor," these critics screamed. The "Viewpoints" section of the *Dallas Morning News* offered this: "Captain Scott O'Grady, bless his hide, is beneficiary of an ancient law of nature. Timing is everything. . . . In old days of Pacific, Korea and Vietnam campaigns, there might be a dozen such adventures every week, or perhaps every day. But we have had none lately, and therefore we had a lot of hero worship stacked up." Mary McGrory satirized the event in the *Washington Post*: "Captain Scott O'Grady, everybody's favorite ant-eater, went to the Pentagon in the pouring rain for a brief ceremony in his honor. Just before he got up to speak, the skies brightened and a glimmer of sun appeared. He's like that. Pure voodoo." An editorial in the *Cincinnati Enquirer* went, "Pardon me, but what's the big deal? . . . Those of us who survived being shot down by the enemy in World War II, we were never considered heroes per se. More likely, fighter pilots were cursed by their commanders for wasting a plane."

Embittered downsizing survivors would more likely identify with this last writer. Rarely are they celebrated for their role as survivors who must carry on the organization. Rarely do they feel supported with the necessary information about why and how they are valued. Seldom do they get the training and re-orientation or the promises needed to feel secure and to make their best contribution.

Instead, downsizing survivors feel overburdened, ignored, unappreciated, and undervalued in most cases. Unlike O'Grady, who himself wondered out loud why he was being given so much attention, downsizing survivors wonder why no one cares about their concerns. These unsung heroes of business and government defend their right to grieve. They wander around like the employees in John Vesta's company, talking about how awful things are and speculating about the worst possible outcomes for their future. As they share the pain of their insecurity and their anxieties, they develop a strong victim identity. And they bond around this identity like the survivors of the African slave trade, Hiroshima, or the Holocaust.

## Excessive Stress

In the most basic sense, stress is a physiological response to a perceived threat, or stressor. It is estimated that, when we are faced with any one stressor, some 1,400 bodily changes occur, all aimed at protecting us by assisting us to flee the situation causing the stress or to fight our way out of it. Most notably, adrenalin and other hormones are released into the bloodstream, causing our metabolism, heart rate, blood pressure, and breathing rate to increase as our muscles tense, getting us ready to act on our own behalf. This response, identified in the early twentieth century by Walter Bradford Cannon of Harvard Medical School as the "fight-or-flight" response, is key to human survival in a sometimes hostile world. In our earliest cave-dwelling beginnings, this primitive response enabled humans to wield their clubs against the wild beasts about to maul them (fight) or to outrun the animals with incredible adrenalin-induced speed (flight). We continue to carry these protective mechanisms with us today, evoking the fight-or-flight response in every stress-provoking situation. We induce the response whether the "wild beast" resides within us as thoughts fueled by deeply held fears or beliefs or whether we are physically stuck in a traffic jam on our way to a job interview. We elicit the response whether we are excessed from our jobs or uneasily survive the cuts.

It is no surprise that in the nineties workplace stress has reached epidemic proportions. Not all of it is related to downsizing, of course. The *Fortune* article "Burned-Out Bosses" suggests that downsizing survivors incur more stress and psychological damage than those laid off and that the increase in disability claims for mental and nervous illnesses since 1989 may be attributed in part to the survivors' experience in the aftermath of downsizing. Researchers around the globe have consistently demonstrated that the physiological changes associated with the fight-or-flight response to stress are linked significantly to stress-related diseases like hypertension, heart disease, and generally lowered resistance to a variety of illnesses. This is why job dissatisfaction is the number one predictor of sudden premature coronary death. And there is no small coincidence in the fact that most on-the-job deaths occur at 9 A.M. on Monday mornings.

In addition to the stress of layoffs, today's employees wrestle with multiple stressors, such as uncertainty about the future, job overload, role ambiguity, and concerns about family and work balance, to name only a few. The physiological responses to these stressors are accompanied by emotional and behavioral ones as well. Emotionally, we observe increased incidences of depression, anxiety, fear, distrust, and all of the other symptoms outlined above. Behaviorally, we observe low productivity, increased absenteeism, workplace violence, sabotaging of self and others, and so forth. These responses are sometimes labeled "burnout." Burned-out bosses and burned-out employees are commonplace today. In a radically downsized manufacturing plant that is one of our clients, workers are logging twelve-hour shifts and often working six to seven days a week. They have resorted to macabre humor to vent their feelings, often talking about the possibility of "going postal" if the pressures continue to escalate.

Clearly, while the fight-or-flight response is useful, it can have harmful effects if it is stimulated constantly, especially in contemporary business and personal settings, where we have few opportunities to fight or flee in a way that enables all systems to return to a normal, relaxed state. The downsizing survivor sitting on the edge of her chair waiting for the next ax to fall experiences physiological, emotional, and behavioral stress responses daily. Yet she cannot pounce on her stressor, brandishing a club on her behalf. Neither can she bolt from the source of her tension, for she is locked in a codependent union with the very organization that causes her stress. So, like Sharon Smallman at Zedco, she capitulates, burying her stress in self-pity and withdrawing to nurse her wounds and tend to her damaged morale.

## FROM CODEPENDENCE TO SELF-SUFFICIENCY

The intensity of the survivor's feelings of pain is exacerbated by two critical, but often overlooked, realities:

- American workers are locked in dependent or codependent relationships with their organizations.
- At the same time, many American workers now see their companies as the oppressor.

It is as if the survivor is locked into a dependent relationship with a suddenly hostile paternal employer. The source of livelihood and economic security now tells the surviving employee, "I can no longer guarantee you a secure future. We are in a crisis, and I may have to make some difficult decisions, like asking you to leave. In the meantime, I need you to be more judicious about your performance. I need to cut costs and work more productively and more efficiently. I need you to put in more time and achieve better quality results in all you do, but even if you are successful, it is possible that you may still have to leave." The survivor responds, not by letting go, not by stepping bravely into the neutral zone of change on his or her way to a new beginning, but by clinging further to the last vestiges of paternal protection.

For some it is a flashback to the dependence and the struggle for independence of our childhood. As babies we all came into the world totally dependent. We then embarked on a life-long process of growth toward independence (becoming self-sustaining) and interdependence (working jointly with others). First we sought sustenance from our mother's breast, and then we learned to sit, pulling ourselves up from a prone position. Next we rolled around from side to side, learning to appreciate our own power. Then we sought autonomous movement, first crawling, then painstakingly, conscientiously attempting our first steps. It was a challenging and bumpy road. We took many falls and made many false starts. But we persisted, sometimes in spite of great physical challenges, seeking competence, seduced by unseen forces that beckoned us toward individuation, mobility, self-sufficiency, and effectiveness in the world. This is a natural, instinctive process for babies (and for adults!).

And yet at some level we learned that we all must depend on others. This interdependence is necessary for our well-being. Even the most self-sufficient among us need people in our lives as we give and receive nurturance, support, or assistance at different times and in different ways. Imagine a culture without parents, teachers, cops, lovers, or nurses. But depending on others is different from being dependent or being codependent.

Dependency implies sustained powerlessness. Codependency is an unhealthy form of dependency. The term, made popular by eighties addiction literature, was originally applied to those relationships in which one, or most likely both, party's self-worth was neurotically tied to meeting the addictive needs of the other. The unspoken pact of the codependent with his or her partner goes like this: "I will enable you to get all of your needs met, even if this is unhealthy for you or for me. Even if it compromises my own values and needs, I will look the other way when you make bad choices. I will remain connected to you for better or worse, and in return I ask that you never forsake me." Bookstores are replete with codependency self-help books whose titles tell the whole story, addressing both the symptoms— "*It Hurts, Don't Stop,*" "*Why Do I Think I'm Nothing Without a Man*"—and the cures— "*Self-Parenting,*" "*Help Yourself,*" "*The Language of Letting Go.*"

The price of codependency is that we learn not to trust ourselves. We define our self-worth in terms of our connection to the other. We come to believe that we cannot survive without them.

Today's employers have decided that they can no longer be in a dependent or codependent relationship with their employees. Driving forces like shareholder demands, technology, global competition, regulatory requirements, and the excesses of the past pose new economic challenges and force tough managerial choices. Some employers handle the cuts badly, severing important contributors and siphoning off talent, cutting too deeply and then having to staff up again, or cutting for foolish reasons such as short-term profits at the expense of long-term losses. Others are justified in making the cuts, having become victims of excesses or having to close down a particular line of business for poor performance or loss of market share. But no matter what the reasons for downsizing, the survivor responses remain predictable. When the organization stance becomes "We can no longer guarantee your employment security," the still codependent employee, not yet ready to change the nature of the relationship, is shocked and betrayed. He or she now sees the employer as the oppressor.

Whenever we are in a codependent relationship with someone we experience as our oppressor, we are in for a lot of pain and disillusionment. Racially oppressed minorities know this well. So do battered spouses and embittered, warring ethnic factions. And so do workers who really believe that the workplace should be a safe haven of employment rights and job security. Low morale and employee rage are compounded by their sense of vulnerability. And while the managers involved, and even members of the senior leadership staff, also experience the pangs of these sweeping changes, their pain is different. As one of America's leading social and cultural thinkers, bell hooks, reminds us, "The rage of the oppressed is never the same as the rage of the privileged. One group can change their lot only by changing the system; the other hopes to be rewarded within the system."

There are many steps management must take to begin to heal their downsizing organizations. These will be the subject of the chapters that follow. Healing cannot begin, however, until the survivors themselves take personal responsibility for their share of the healing process.

The survivor perceptions, feelings, and behaviors discussed so far are normal for any human being facing dramatic change or losses. We all go through denial, anger, grief, insecurity, and confusion as we confront life's challenges and the ups and downs of work life. But within each group of survivors there are those who emerge as victors, true heroes of the conditions they endure, versus those who remain stuck in a "victim identity," rather than being true survivors. The key lies in how we relate to our pain and to the object or source of our pain. Victims have difficulty moving away from dependence, from codependence, or from counterdependent attacks on the object of their pain, all of which are maladaptive stances. True survivors move toward independence—a restored sense of self and interdependence with other members of their group. These are positive stances from which stem power and effectiveness.

Survivor bonding and victim identity are not unusual. As pointed out earlier, we observe these phenomenon among African Americans who survived slavery, among Japanese who survived the bombing of Hiroshima, and among Jews who survived the Holocaust. And we observe it in reaction to workplace losses.

Healing, however, begins only when survivors find ways to break the chains of dependence, take steps to heal their self-esteem, and proactively adopt strategies to cocreate their own future.

Based on years of research, the psychologist Al Siebert, author of *The Survivor Personality*, developed a definition of the survivor that he explains in a chapter entitled "Life Is Not Fair—And That Can Be Very Good for You." He offers four criteria that define survivor types. They

- "have survived a major crisis or challenge;
- surmounted the crisis through personal effort;
- emerged from the experience with previously unknown strengths and abilities; and
- afterwards find value in the experience."

By this definition, the term "survivor" applied to employees who remain after layoffs is a misnomer for some. Many often feel more like victims. Many do not believe that they can rise above the crisis through personal will. They do not ask, What are the lessons this experience holds for me? or How can I re-create my experience of work? Rather, they wonder, Where will I get the support to allay my fears and rekindle my motivation? Why should I work harder to fill the void left by colleagues when no one cares about my needs? They feel unappreciated, undervalued, and even violated.

I'm reminded of a friend whom I will call Maynard Coleman. His graduation at the top of his class from Texas A&M University came as a surprise to no one. He was a fast-tracker, a mover and shaker. His ego, pride, and sense of self were exceeded only by his generosity and his trust in humankind. He was a positive thinker who decided at age eight that he wanted to be a "space pioneer." At ages nine and ten, he won first place two years running in the Charles Drew Science Competition, a program designed to interest minorities in the sciences. At age seventeen he won a full scholarship to the college of his choice. He breezed through each class, applying himself with great vigor and discipline. He just knew that he would land a job in the aerospace industry upon earning his master's degree in engineering. And he did. He landed his dream job on his second interview. "Maynard Coleman, Research Associate," his new business card greeted him two weeks after he had joined the most coveted R&D group in the business. Then, two years later, at the peak of his new career, the cuts came. They were mandatory. They were across the board. Anyone was fair game.

The first wave of depression swept over Coleman quite unexpectedly one day as he sat in his lab office across from the empty desk of a former colleague, Dolores Williams, who had chosen to "quit before I'm laid off." Dolores had defiantly taken her life's savings and bought a franchised business. Occasionally she would call him up and joke, "There's life out here! Get out while you can still walk!" Dolores had been a brilliant lab technician, a humorous, high-energy colleague who was impatient with bureaucracy and who delighted in bucking the system. But still, why would she leave voluntarily? he wondered. Her job, like his, was fairly well protected, for both worked in an area declared a "core competency." They worked on top secret technologies that were critical to the organization's future, and they had both received technical training that made their expertise virtually invaluable at the moment.

This first wave of depression startled Coleman. He had always been a trooper. Clouds with silver linings were his thing, yet now these feelings settled in around him like a dank blanket of fear and sadness. During those moments his thoughts often turned to his fiancée, Tanika Cooper, and their plans for the future. She was in her fifth year of undergraduate school, having changed her career goals and her major four times. But she was a great student and was driven to succeed. That was one thing they had in common. What made them different was that she was a drifter, an explorer. He knew, had always known, what he wanted. He loved engineering and in particular the research end of things. He craved the thrill of conquering "unsolvable" problems through scientific inquiry. In fact, the more insecure the employment outlook became, the more he lost himself in the computer simulations that were the mainstay of his work.

A year earlier his colleague Jack Kublack had stopped by his office and announced, "Rumor has it there's going to be an-other wave of cuts. Second quarter results are in. We didn't make the numbers." Another wave of depression swept over Coleman, this time joined by an angry edge that he wore on his sleeve when I met him later that week at a professional net-working event.

"So you're a management consultant," he observed, mildly cynical yet mildly interested in what insights I might have to of-fer informally. "There's a lot of those running around our or-ganization these days with all the downsizing and changes going on. I hate what you guys have done to the name of my field, calling what you do reengineering." The pain peeped through his protest.

"Well, I see you are one of the lucky survivors." Sarcasm met sarcasm as I defended my field, and a great friendship was awk-wardly conceived. We spoke for a long time about survivors and victims, management and leadership, the "demise" of big business, the changes in government, the implications for ed-ucation, and on and on.

Over the next five years I kept in touch with Coleman. He would call to chat and get informal advice from a colleague who consults with rapidly changing organizations. He would share the latest about how he and his restructured organization were coming along. He complained about the escalating work-load and about the work losing its joy because of politics. He worried about the constant outsourcing of more and more jobs to independent contractors, whom he felt didn't always care about the best interests of the organization. He confided his growing depression and the breakup of his engagement be-cause he "just wasn't sure about the future anymore." Then one day, after playing long-distance therapist for half an hour, I wearily asked the question that marked a critical turning point for Coleman.

"Well, Maynard, why do you think you survived the cuts?"

"Because I'm invaluable to this outfit and they know it!" he retorted instantly. "I do what I do better than anyone, even in my lowest moments. I'm good at what I do, I'm creative, I'm always upgrading my skills, and even though I worry about the consequences, I'm still the kind of guy that tells it like it is. I've championed more ideas throughout this organization in three years than most scientists do in a lifetime. Sometimes they shake their heads in disbelief. They can't believe how good I am at what I do. I can't believe it myself sometimes."

I could hear his former indomitable ego and self-esteem returning. He was energized now, on a roll. "Stay with that feeling," I offered, poking fun at psychotherapists. He laughed openly for the first time in months, getting the point. "I'm serious," I insisted, "you need to stay with that feeling. Repeat those facts to yourself and to your supervisor if she hasn't noticed. Remind yourself daily of what you have to offer, there or elsewhere if necessary."

Coleman's depression was, of course, linked to his codependence with his organization. He had hired on with high hopes for a secure future. When he concluded that the future was uncertain, his feelings of fear, based on his dependence, sapped his spirit and threatened to drain his energy. He became reenergized that day during our discussion when he got in touch with the source of his personal power and his value to the organization. In fact, what had kept him going and allowed him to remain a star performer was the stimulation and results he got from training, risk taking, and an entrepreneurial bent that he had been out of touch with until that moment. Were it not for these fortunate personal traits, he could have easily become totally demotivated and ineffective. His new awareness of his personal power put him in a good position to do what he must to truly survive: break the chains of his dependence on and codependence with the organization.

Given today's economic climate, no one could predict the future of Maynard Coleman's career in his organization. His entire division could be eliminated for reasons beyond his control. The work he does could cease to be a core area for the business because of shifts in marketplace demands. The costs of production might escalate to the point that the organization could no longer compete. Or the worst-case scenario could occur. Customers, who, by the way, are a lot more willing to change than organizations are, might simply leave and go where they could get better value for their money, putting Coleman and every one in his organization out of business.

But we do know one thing. Coleman's attitude about training would keep him competitive for a long time. This is especially true in fields like engineering, where skills become obsolete almost as soon as a person learns them. American business spends over $200 billion annually—more than the total U.S. public education budget from kindergarten through college—on workforce training. This need will only escalate as the global economy drives the need for more highly skilled workers. It is alarming that, currently, the U.S. ranks fourteenth among the sixteen or so major industrial countries in its investment in public education. Workers entering the U.S. workforce often lack the skills they need to survive with such increasingly competitive entities as a reunified Germany, a powerful Pacific Rim, and a more and more integrated European economy. American schools, like the government and businesses, are restructuring and reinventing themselves to forge new alliances aimed at preparing workers for this reality.

Survivors and survivor managers in every sector must become equal partners in reshaping the future of the workplace so that the needs of workers, customers, shareholders, and employers are met. Both must work together to break down bureaucratic barriers as well as classism and the other systemic isms that block the inclusion and full participation of the workforce in shaping the decisions affecting its members. The survivor's challenge is how to develop the technical and emotional skills to reinvent work and restore the employee/employer relationship to a healthier state. This is crucial as managers and supervisors begin to share problem-solving and decision-making power with the rest of the workforce in order to capture the talents and ideas needed to remain competitive. It is the key to renegotiating a social contract that is empower-

ing and effective in allowing the survivor to pursue meaningful, lucrative work. I will discuss specific ideas for doing so in
chapter 10.

—✺—

## SURVIVOR CLOSE-UP

Not one to put all his eggs in one basket, Audley Williams, a
telecommunications engineer with a New York bank, decided
to take his career into his own hands. He had lived through a
merger of Chemical Bank and Manufacturers Hanover Trust
that required downsizing and restructuring. When rumors hit
that there was the likelihood of another merger with Chase
Manhattan, this loyal long-term employee reassessed his career options and decided that to weather the stormy banking
industry he had to become a marketable commodity rather
than a dependent employee.

> Today's employees can no longer be complacent. They live in
> a competitive marketplace. That means being the best you can.
> Having the highest skill levels so you can remain current is the
> key. The only people that will survive are those who are willing
> to learn new skills and those who are not afraid of change. To
> my mind it's counterproductive to ignore what's going on
> around you. When your managers start to express their doubts
> about the future of your group, it's time to rethink your options.
> In my former job meetings became a series of one-way infor-
> mational forums in which they told us what's going on and
> what to prepare ourselves for. That atmosphere began to crip-
> ple some employees as they started making bets about who
> would leave and how many would be laid off.

In a supposedly cost-saving move, Chase Manhattan had
negotiated an eight-year, $56 million deal in which AT&T ac-
quired Chase's telecommunications function and its employees and then contracted them back to Chase Manhattan. By
industry standards this looked like a bargain. But on a per-user

basis, as each person was hooked up to the network, Chase Manhattan was assessed additional fees above and beyond the initial contract. This represented the death cry of corporate America: redundant costs. When Chase and Chemical Bank later merged, they inherited this arrangement. The Chase workers were indispensable—they carried the expertise of the telecommunications function. Chemical Bank's dilemma became Do we become victims of this contract, laying off our telecommunications employees to cut costs, or do we go to bat for them? Chemical decided to take a stand.

They told us, "Don't worry; we'll take a stand for you." This raised the question of trust for us employees. Many of us were afraid to test the waters of trust, so we began looking around for jobs. It was energizing for me to explore my worth in the marketplace. I continued to feel positive about my current job, because as I explored other options I knew I was not trapped. I never became one of those anxious, insecure employees who worry about their future daily.

The telecommunications industry is moving away from the IBM mainframe environment to the PC world of client-server applications. This allows work groups to share services simultaneously, thereby increasing efficiency and reducing costs. I saw this trend as an opportunity to reposition myself in the industry. I now see myself as a commodity with an index of skills upon which any company can draw. When I announced my decision to leave, my manager understood and wished me luck because they knew they couldn't compete with a counteroffer or the promise of a stable future.

In his new position with another leading New York bank, Williams faces the daily reality that his bank could be acquired.

This is the new reality. Knowing this, my colleagues and I who are into lifelong learning are relatively fearless. Next week I'm off for another round of training on the latest iteration of leading-edge Internet technology. I'll come back even more competitive than before. As a marketable commodity, my goal is to expose myself to as much training as possible. I love my work. It's exciting, challenging, and satisfying to know that I am making a lasting impact on the world by being a key player in the telecommunications industry.

## Chapter 3

—◇◇◇—

# THE MANAGER'S CHALLENGE: RESTORING TRUST

" 'Let go, or be let go!' That's what I've been telling my supervisees lately. I'm tired. I'm tired of employees acting as though I'm responsible for their morale." We were standing around the coffee machine on a break during a leadership session in a perpetually downsizing company. The session included managers and technical professionals in a joint session titled "From Surviving to Thriving."

The concerned frown on my brow evoked a rush of guilt. So the manager went on to explain himself further:

Look, we have been downsizing every year since 1986. Some cuts are good. We have reduced many unnecessary management layers. In some cases we really did cut excess fat. Some cuts were not so good, like our "across-the-board formulas," or when we jumped on the outsourcing bandwagon and lost two of our best customers because they felt service was being compromised, or when we cut excessively, then had to upsize some of our departments. But these are the realities, and people need to lighten up and accept these changes. We all suffer from anxiety, but at some point employees have got to realize that the company is not here to make them feel good. We're here to get a job done.

He stopped, slightly out of breath. Then he asked, "What do you think, Delorese?"

My mind was elsewhere. I was thinking of the communication that another client had just sent out to surviving employees with this message: "Some of you have begun to confuse feeling good with doing a good job. We are not here to make you feel good. We are here to help you become all you can be—to achieve excellence. It would be nice if you felt good, but it is not necessary."

Before I could answer, a second manager, overhearing our conversation, chimed in, "I see it differently. Downsizing is a life event. Like any other loss, a grieving process is needed. The problem as I see it is a loss of self-esteem. People no longer feel like they are worth anything. We owe it to them to help them get past that."

A third manager interrupted. "I disagree. People have got to take responsibility for their own healing. Managers can only do so much. The rest is up to the employee. I can't give somebody self-esteem."

"Let's get Bev and Allan into this conversation," the second manager suggested, as he motioned for the administrative assistant and an engineer, neither of whom was a manager, to join what was becoming a heated debate. "You overheard what we've been talking about. What do you think?"

They hesitantly moved closer. Allan, the brilliant engineer-turned-cynic, offered, "There's not much I can add to this discussion. I no longer have any expectations about anything. I hardly see my manager anyway—she's always off somewhere managing—something. I just do my job and go home."

Bev was a bit more gracious. She, still somewhat tentative about telling her truth to a group of managers, suggested, "Well, I don't expect my supervisor to make me happy, but he sure is capable of making my life here real unhappy. Not that he does," she added quickly, covering herself from any possible retribution. "But it's hard when they [managers] make inconsiderate decisions that make our work life unbearable, then turn around and ask us to be 'empowered' and to be 'team players.'"

Noticing my furious note taking at this point, the first manager, deciding to bring the debate to a close, added, "Well, Delorese, if you're planning on putting this in your book, make sure you tell both sides of the story."

I was not really convinced that there were two sides to the story. Clearly, there are two sets of organizational roles and responsibilities for survivor employees and survivor managers. But I was very much aware that most of the managers I work with are themselves wounded survivors, subject to the same feelings of anxiety and betrayal as other employees. It was clear to me that in this case the managers' syndrome was compounded by a growing exasperation at not really knowing how to go about creating a work climate that supported healing in the aftermath of downsizing.

When I shared my observations with the frustrated manager, he acquiesced somewhat. "Yeah, well, you might have a point there. But this is a crisis for heaven's sake! If we're all survivors in this together, let's get on with it!"

So, from the viewpoint of the manager who invokes the admonition "Let go, or be let go!" the lucky survivor needs to come on board quickly. In this manager's mind there is no time for wound licking or whimpering about the pain of lost security and overwork. The surviving employee must move directly from loss to a new beginning.

William Bridges has made a magnificent contribution to our understanding of the process of moving through loss to new beginnings. A leading expert on managing human and organizational transitions, Bridges makes an important distinction between change and transition. He describes change as a part of objective reality—the inevitable and necessary adjustments we face in the course of our lives as we move to a new job or devise new technology or are beset by new competition. Transition, he explains, is the psychological process people must work through as they come to accept change. In his book *Managing Transitions: Making the Most of Change*, he offers the kicker "It isn't the changes that do you in, it's the transitions."

Transition, paradoxically, begins with an ending—a letting go of what was familiar. This enables us to move to, in Bridges words, "the neutral zone . . . the no-man's-land between the old reality and the new . . . the limbo between the old sense of identity and the new . . . when the old way is gone and the new doesn't feel comfortable yet." In this neutral ground the individual or organization in transition finds both the challenge and the opportunity for creative change. It represents a sort of gestation period in which people are afforded the chance to emerge phoenixlike out of the ashes of their losses to enjoy an inspired rebirth—a new beginning.

This transition from ending to neutral zone to new beginning cannot be rushed. It must be fully experienced and worked through deliberately, and sometimes painstakingly, if the individual and the organization are to heal themselves. The mistake that individuals and organizations typically make is to dash headlong into the new beginning without allowing the process of transition to follow its natural path to healing.

"Let go, or be let go!" This seemingly heartless cry of a survivor manager, himself in pain, reveals the frustration of leading and managing change in the face of possible extinction. The manager's challenge to lead employees to a new beginning in the aftermath of cuts and reorganization is compounded even further by the survivors' inability to let go and move forward. Their codependence on the organization, a source of their well-being in the first place, becomes a barrier. Lowered morale, work overload, and uncertainty about the future become major obstacles to letting go and moving forward.

Faced with the final accountability for the organization's future, managers don't often have the time or the patience to build a work environment that heals losses and supports the emotional component of transition. Like the managers in the above example, the Humex Corporation's managers felt that the employees were unreasonably ignoring the business challenges that were driving the necessary changes. For them the barrage of survivor complaints were interpreted as a lack of sensitivity to market conditions and the company's plight.

While they were vaguely concerned about the possibility that the workforce would initially experience anxiety, they were more interested in getting employees to let go and embrace a new beginning. The sooner the better.

It wasn't that management was totally oblivious to the human dynamics of downsizing. In fact, in planning meetings John Vesta and other senior managers talked frequently about the inevitability of employees' resistance to change. They anticipated that the transition would result in lost morale and that people would be disoriented and frustrated for a while. The management team also briefly discussed the possible impact of the employees' dissatisfaction on productivity and customer service. But none of this was ever broached with employees. Not once did management concede, "I know this is difficult for you." In all of management's interactions with employees, the communications were primarily about "refocusing on the future" and "making the numbers."

Managers were convinced that, once survivors embraced this new reality, things would return to normal and the company would regain momentum, outperforming the previous year. So, while they anticipated some employee discomfort, Vesta and his staff were captured by the more immediate challenge of cutting spending, getting the products out the door, and making the targeted return on investment. Unfortunately, by failing to pay sufficient attention to the letting-go process before attempting to align survivors with the new direction and goals, they rushed headlong down a path that led to several tactical errors.

## COMMON TACTICAL ERRORS

### Poor Management Communication

Humex's management communicated information about the layoffs and related activities, as well as the new vision and goals, en masse through E-mail and company memos and piecemeal in various staff meetings. Employees got more or less information, with more or less accuracy, depending on the whims and personalities of their immediate supervisors. Overall, Humex employees got insufficient details about the changes. They had no concept of how the layoffs and proposed restructuring fit into the bigger organizational picture or into the external environment in which the company functioned competitively. As a result they had several misperceptions about how the layoffs were handled, what the business case for the decision was, and what impact these decisions would have on the organization's future. In their informal communications with one another, they compared notes and shared conflicting viewpoints about these matters. In the absence of consistent, detailed, and accurate facts, their rumor mill processed information that was distorted and ultimately demoralizing.

Foremost among employee concerns was the fact that there was insufficient or conflicting information about the general manager's vision and goals. They interpreted this to mean that the senior leadership team was unsure about the future of the organization. This led employees to speculate about whether the general manager really knew what he was doing or really cared about their issues and concerns. Further, because the flow of communication was one-way, with little opportunity for two-way dialogue, employee feedback, venting of feelings, or question-and-answer forums, employees were forced into a compliance mode. They felt that they were expected to "listen up," to get the message and do as they were told. They were left with the distinct impression that all that mattered was making the numbers.

In the meantime the general manager was doing a pretty good job of communicating with his staff of middle managers. They had become a close-knit team in many respects. They bonded together as targets of the employees' ire and frustrations. They became sounding boards for one another. John Vesta regularly involved this team of nine managers in brainstorming and planning sessions for creating innovative solutions to the many challenges they still faced. But underlying their communication choices down through the organization was the mistaken assumption that employees had no need to know all the details at this point. As Vesta himself put it, "We don't want to unnecessarily raise expectations by painting too rosy a picture of our plans for the future." So while, for the most part, Vesta and his staff felt positive about the future and confident that they could turn things around, they thought it best to take a more muted approach to communication. Somehow, even the messages they thought were important to share were not reaching the general workforce as intended. Or, if they were, these messages were not being embraced fully. While managers felt that they communicated the right messages quite effectively, employees experienced confusion and alienation from the message and from the process.

This is a typical scenario in today's restructuring organizations. In the case of Humex, there was an almost exclusive focus on short-term business profit and winning in the marketplace. Little concern was shown for the emotional, physical, and professional well-being of those charged with making the numbers and "winning the war." Surviving employees were given pep talks and new performance targets to shoot for but no time or forum to deal with their anxieties and grieve their losses. In a letter sent to each employee three weeks after the layoffs and restructuring process, Vesta expressed the following message:

> I want to thank each and every one of you for your commitment, your courage, and your support during the transition we have just experienced. You are the backbone of this organization; you are our most valued assets. The competition is fierce and times are challenging, but we are encouraged because we have world-class employees like you. Your greatest potential lies ahead. You have the capacity to outperform the best. We are counting on you to move forward with the vision and goals set forth in our "World Class Leadership 2000" planning document, which you have all received in summary form by now. Your supervisors will be using this planning document to guide

your performance objectives and your work activities over the next several years.

The document was masterfully done. Vesta and his management team had spent several weeks in planning retreats with top-notch design and communications experts creating the plan and setting it forth in a glossy four-color brochure. He assumed that the plan was being embraced by managers and employees alike. How could they not? It was clear, inspiring, doable, and well thought out.

What management did not realize was that, in the absence of a climate of healing, in the presence of unacknowledged confusion, loss, and pain, employees simply perceived the "World Class Leadership 2000" visioning activity as additional pressure to achieve without adequate support and resources.

## Management Denial

If denial is a trap for survivor employees in downsizing organizations, it is an even bigger trap for the managers charged with leading the changes. In fact, the higher up the managerial ladder, the greater the potential for denial. Perhaps the most telling evidence of managerial denial was Humex's failure to plan ahead for survivor issues. John Vesta was genuinely shocked when he received the consultants' feedback from his employee focus groups. Somehow he had deluded himself into thinking that the disorientation of the layoffs and restructuring would be a momentary event, followed by a restoration of trust and morale and a return to business as usual. Denial was evident when the Humex management gave employees assurances that "things would certainly get better with the proper level of cooperation" and that the "likelihood of further layoffs was virtually none." Interestingly, employees were given few specific facts, figures, or projections to substantiate these claims.

As employees worked past their own initial denial to confront their losses, they surmised, and rightly so, that the promise of stability was one that management might not be able to keep in today's business environment. Questioning the willingness and ability of management to take care of their needs, employees began to put their lives on hold. They canceled the purchase of new cars. They begin to shore up their savings. Many canceled family vacations or postponed plans for moving to a larger home as they waited to see what happened.

On the Humex consultants' survey, 76 percent reported high turnover intent by checking "strongly agree" to the statement "I would leave tomorrow if a new job came along." Several circulated their resumes externally, and some left for new, hopefully more secure, jobs. Interestingly, managerial denial was also reflected in the findings of this survey. When asked to indicate their views on employees' turnover intent, managers, on average, answered that they thought 25 percent of their employees might be thinking of leaving. The survey data revealed that the higher up the organization one went the greater the level of this kind of denial. In the seniormost ranks some indicated that they thought 10 percent of the employees might be thinking of leaving.

## Lack of Retraining and Reorientation

Every change involves a loss of prior competence, a loss of prior identity, and general disorientation. This is especially true after downsizing, when many employees are given expanded job responsibilities without additional skill training. By focusing exclusively on the long-term goals of cutting costs, the Humex management failed to consider the important short-term investment in skills training needed to ensure continuity. Employees were being asked to make decisions differently, do work in areas that were new to many, exercise new leadership skills, and in some cases become comfortable with new procedures and technology. All of these activities required additional training and coaching that was attained piecemeal, rather than being planned for. The inevitable losses of organizational change—disorientation, disidentification, insecurity, job ambiguity, work overload—were compounded by a lack of education and training. For Humex employees this translated into heightened anxiety, lowered productivity, and a tendency to take fewer risks and show less initiative.

## Diminished Rewards and Resources

In every case employees at Humex were given expanded responsibilities without additional compensation or resources. The sales force was traveling more and carrying up to twice the customer load in some cases. Everyone, especially supervisory personnel, was spending more time in meetings. Technical and support people complained that they were typically on their own and were required to take on more and more decision-making and problem-solving responsibilities without additional compensation. Employees saw this as a glaring inequity. It reinforced their sense of being underappreciated and exploited. Again, in thinking about cost savings, the Humex management had failed to see the inevitable costs of eliminating performance rewards.

In addition to drastic budget cuts, many support jobs deemed to be nonessential to business operations, although they were helpful to the technical and managerial staff, were eliminated. At the same time the remaining employees were being asked to do more. Again, the experience of being asked to do more with less played into feelings of exploitation. In addition, this exacerbated the level of work-related stress.

## Failure to Manage Cultural Clash

A clash of cultures does not only occur when two different organizations come together through mergers or acquisitions. Cultural clash also occurs when an organization adopts a new way of doing business without letting go of old assumptions. An organization's culture evolves as its managers and employees adopt a shared set of values, norms, and behaviors that have consistently served the organization in solving day-to-day challenges. Culture therefore becomes a proven survival tool over time, as tried and true values, norms, and behavior become frozen as part of the organization's unconscious belief system. These matters are driven deep into people's psyches and become taken for granted as "the way things are done around here." Because the culture has successfully ensured the organization's survival and success in the past, it serves to maintain the status quo well into the future. As such, the culture itself becomes a restraining force against change long after new conditions and challenges beg for new solutions.

Unwittingly, John Vesta and his management team had set out to create a new organizational culture without fully understanding the organization's existing culture and the underlying assumptions that would pose barriers to change. There was no plan for overcoming resistance to cultural change or for creating a new culture that would support the restructured organization and its strategic intent. Supervisors were generally ill prepared to interpret the culture; assess survivor needs; educate them about the new vision, values, goals, priorities, and expectations for the restructured organization; and establish incentives and a plan for true cultural change. The net result of this was that, in addition to problems like distrust and anxiety, employees labored under old assumptions about the nature of the work and the workplace, the nature of the employee/employer relationship, and the nature of the business environment, none of which was any longer appropriate.

With these common tactical errors in mind, let us look more specifically at the manager's challenge in healing the downsized organization.

## THE MANAGER'S CHALLENGE

John Vesta's story reminds us that leading and managing the downsized organization is no easy task. There was a time when managers knew how to act. There was a neat chain of com-

mand displayed on carefully designed organizational charts. A
manager knew who reported directly to him. They showed up
for work, punched in or logged in, reported to their worksta-
tions, and followed the supervisor's orders. The manager's job
was to plan, organize, monitor, and control the activities of
people who basically did what they were told. Now Vesta and
thousands of managers like him are not so sure how to negotiate the rapids of change. Managers face an enormous identity
crisis in their downsizing, restructuring world. It is a crisis
rooted in paradoxes, moral dilemmas, and competing demands. It is a cultural clash between business realities and
newly espoused values.

Consider the following examples generated by participants
in my leadership seminars:

| THE BUSINESS REALITIES | THE ESPOUSED VALUES |
|---|---|
| Be a warrior; wield a cost-cutting ax. | Be a healer, a trusted coach. |
| Don't fail; it's costly. | Take risks; innovate. |
| Expect longer work hours. | Promote family and life balance. |
| Shrink the workforce. | Grow the profits. |
| Survive short-term; work harder. | Think long-term; work smarter. |
| Maintain stability. | Be a visionary leader of change. |

Each of these dilemmas challenges the soul of the harangued
worker and the harried manager in a workplace defined by
sweeping changes. Unresolved, they lead to the number one
leadership problem managers face today—a loss of trust.

## Be a Warrior and a Healer

Today's conventional business wisdom teaches that the enlightened manager is a coach. To most of us this conjures up
visions of someone wise who mentors, guides, instructs, and
calls forth our finest talents as team players. A coach is also
someone we trust to have our best interests at heart and to in-
tervene on our behalf. Because he is an instigator of high per-

formance, the coach's primary charge is to create conditions that equip and inspire players to win.

Yet, in the minds of many employees, the coach is becoming the enemy. Having landed the role of manager, the coach also belongs to a body of decision makers now charged with cutting people to reduce overhead. "Don't call us team players," angry layoff survivors in one of my focus groups asked of their managers, "and don't call yourselves coaches; this is not a game." The distrust and feelings of betrayal in this employee group were matched by the frustration of the harried managers receiving the feedback: "What do they want from us? We're doing the best we can given the business realities."

## Don't Fail but Take Risks

Today's managers live huddled in the shadow of possible extinction from the competition. They know that to work harder, faster, and better they must hit the mark accurately the first time, most of the time. With economic predators waiting around the next bend, there is little margin for error. To survive they must outperform the best. This means taking the risks necessary to innovate.

Yet, the will to innovate is anesthetized by the price of failure. When resources are scarce, workers are understandably reluctant to risk new undertakings that may give the organization an edge in the marketplace if successful but cost the organization dearly if they fail. This is compounded by the paradox that the tools of innovation themselves are now often under attack. Time, training, and R&D—opportunities to think and tinker— are often the first casualties in a downsizing environment.

## Expect Longer Work Hours and Promote Balance

One consulting assignment required me and my associates to implement a program that would help employees come to terms with the business realities that called for twelve-hour shifts. At the same time we were to install a stress management workshop that would give participants better coping skills for juggling the demands of work and family life. As we talked with representatives from labor and management, it became clear that everyone agreed on one point. The work hours were becoming excessive. Yet, there was a strong corporate mandate to top the previous year's performance while lowering the cost of doing business. The plant had downsized its workforce, consolidated several operations for greater efficiency, and was doing well—but not well enough yet. Employees talked to us in metaphors about "pressure cookers" and people being on a "short fuse." Managers acknowledged the growing tension caused by unrelenting work hours and expressed concern about burnout and safety issues due to exhaustion. But they were quick to offer the ironic observation that the workforce had become so used to bloated overtime checks that, even though they complained about overwork, they would be equally outraged if they lost the opportunity for extra pay.

In one stress management session an employee offered the following observation, which sums up the quandary many of us find ourselves in today and perhaps have for decades: "It's as though my family life, vacation time, and sleep have become interruptions of work!"

### Shrink the Workforce and Grow the Profits

In the halls of downsizing organizations everywhere managers today ask the question "How much is too much in the way of cutbacks?" When does an organization reach the point of diminishing returns, at which it can no longer do more with less? Those who have mastered the reengineering revolution warn us that invasive surgery may be avoided if we overhaul work processes before we cut people. By itself, they tell us, downsizing can be a major mistake.

While cutting employees is a way to cut costs, it may not reposition the organization more competitively and it may do little to guarantee profits. This is why most companies that downsize do it again and again in wave after wave. And these slashes, ironically, are often followed by waves of rehiring. The 1994 American Management Association study cited in the introduction concludes that within two years 60 percent of downsizing companies rehire to fill vacated positions. From a reengineering perspective the most important measure is satisfaction of customer need. Managers must therefore measure the results of business processes in terms of customer satisfaction, not short-term dollars saved by cutting employees. This is the surest way to grow the profits in the long run.

## Survive Short-Term but Think Long-Term

Government regulations, technological advancements, global competition, shifting customer demands—no one can deny these pressing forces for change in every sector. The adaptive organization must think quickly on its feet to stay in business, and it must carefully reinvent itself for a more competitive future in a rapidly changing world. Today, survival calls for both speedy short-term interventions, often involving more work, and strategic long-term changes, involving smart innovations.

The managers I consult with tell me, "I have no time for thoughtful strategic thinking at the end of a busy day consumed with fighting fires." I tell them that they must restructure their priorities and make the time to reengineer their work processes and engage employees in becoming collaborative shapers of the organization's future. But this is easier said than done, and it remains one of the difficult managerial dilemmas of organizations that are becoming leaner.

## Maintain Stability and Lead Change

Managing and leading are different, sometimes opposing, activities. Good management involves containing costs and increasing outputs to create a stable, profitable organization based on greater efficiency. Good leadership involves upsetting the applecart in order to "unfreeze" and transform the organization for greater effectiveness. Today's effective manager must simultaneously maintain the organization's stability and lead organizational change to ensure future viability.

The paradox lies in understanding that leading changes such as downsizing and restructuring for the future create chaos for the managers and other survivors charged with making things happen. This can threaten productivity, efficiency, and profitability if not handled well. For the survivor manager leading and managing are a delicate balancing act. To err on either side is fatal.

In many respects the managers for whom this book is written are no different from the employee survivors for whom this book is written. The managers are themselves survivors of downsizing. They too experience the feelings of insecurity and anxiety associated with change. And the suggestions for employees, offered at the end of chapter 2, apply to managers as well. Managers, however, differ from other survivors in one important aspect: as sponsors and agents of change, they are held responsible and accountable for the decision to downsize and for the final outcomes of that decision.

The successes I have observed so far have taught me that the following commitments are a good place to start in creating a renewed, motivating environment:

- Communicate with integrity.
- Balance "warrior" acts with acts of healing.
- Manage yourself to lead others.
- Move from "us versus them" to "we."
- Move from win-lose to win-win.
- Be courageous by taking a stand, but be willing to modify your position if necessary.
- Build trust by embracing truth.
- Be honest about current realities and positive about future possibilities.
- Become an expert in cultural change.
- Provide the resources and support that enable employees to continue to perform maximally, both emotionally and tangibly.

- Provide training and lifelong learning opportunities for oneself and others.
- Encourage a movement from surviving to thriving.
- Become comfortable with being uncomfortable.
- Set outrageous goals, plan for success, and celebrate every milestone.

## FROM SURVIVING TO THRIVING
### THE MANAGER'S CHECKLIST

*Communicate with Integrity*

Successful survivor managers are exemplary communicators. They communicate the present realities and the vision for the future, along with values, goals, expectations, and priorities. They do so frequently and clearly and through every medium available. According to studies done by James Kouzes and Barry Posner, the number one expectation that followers have of leaders is honesty. This is especially important during transitions, when people are thrown up into the air, so to speak. The employees fall at different points along a continuum, some moving away from the proposed changes, others moving toward them. The goal of the manager-leader is to align employees so that everyone is moving in the direction of change. Communication becomes a key part of the equation. Through constant, open communication, manager-leaders must explain the present state accurately and honestly. They must then articulate the vision in a convincing, engaging manner and describe the ideal end state so that people want to go there and know the criteria for assessing whether they have arrived. They must communicate values and goals, but more importantly they must model the way. In all communication efforts manager-leaders must walk the talk such that their rhetoric and behavior are consistent. Communicating with survivors cannot effectively be carried out after the fact. It should occur during the early planning phases, during the layoffs, and afterward. Good managerial communication also includes two-way dialogue. Manager-leaders must ask for input, listen, and where practical integrate the feedback they receive from the survivors and customers. This two-way dialogue should be conducted so that it becomes part of the healing process.

Here are some proven pointers:

- Be clear and unambiguous at all times.
- Give lots of information about the changes. And be redundant; say it over and over through every communications medium available.
- Be consistent in your message, and if you change your mind, say so.
- Get off the fence—avoid nonstatements, double negatives, half-truths, and sugarcoating.
- Speak honestly about the losses and the gains.
- Ask for input and feedback. Ask "How am I doing?" And don't shoot the messenger if you dislike what you hear. Avoid yes-men.
- Catch people doing things right and express appreciation.

### Balance "Warrior" Acts with Acts of Healing

Leading and managing downsizing and other changes require tough, decisive "warrior" acts. There is no escaping this. Cutting costs, laying off personnel, eliminating resources—all cause anguish both for the agent of change and the targets of change. This creates an enormous amount of managerial and employee stress that must be resolved before an organization's members can fully commit themselves to the future.

For the manager acts of healing include developing and applying leadership competence; telling the truth even if it hurts at first; letting go of the familiar comfort zone; soliciting honest feedback; providing a forum for grieving for oneself and others; coaching, training, involving, supporting, and enlisting others and enabling them to act; showing patience; and celebrating successes.

Smart managers are not intimidated by the predictable reactions and complaints following change. They understand that there are real losses and real anguish connected with change. The managers in the success stories gathered in this book all provided communication forums at which survivors could express their grief, anger, and disillusionment. Some even scheduled grieving sessions and ritualized the letting-go process so that employees could move to the resolution of their pain.

Finally, the most important act of healing for the manager is the capacity to demonstrate enthusiasm for the future. No one follows a pessimist. If you don't believe in the organization's future, you shouldn't try to lead others there.

## Manage Yourself to Lead Others

Following the execution of downsizing, managers must heal— first themselves and then the other survivors—and then the organization itself can begin to heal. Like the airline safety rule that reminds us to attend first to our own needs in an emergency before assisting others, managers must come to terms with their own needs and the fears that may block them from seeking input, engaging in full, honest dialogue with employees, and developing the attributes of courage and honesty and the skills of leading and motivating. The airline example is in no way an attempt to draw an analogy between parenting and managing—that was the old organizational paradigm. Rather, the point is that managers must first see to their own survival needs and their skills for managing and leading change before they can adequately fulfill their leadership role of modeling the way for workers to move from merely surviving to thriving.

Writing on the subject of healing, Elisabeth Kübler-Ross listed four essential qualities of a healer: trust, faith, love, and humility. Then she added, "Healers must understand that love does not only mean love for others; it also means love for one-self. We must be aware of our limits and know when it is necessary to nurture ourselves. . . . No one can heal without being healed. . . ."

## *Move from "Us Versus Them" to "We"*

A culture of blame, in which each level blames the next, is de-motivating. Inertia results as people fixate on who is to blame rather than on what happened and what can be done to improve results. Promoting "weness" leads to healthy collaboration and teamwork. In such a climate healing begins as people learn to experience the presence of "grace" in the workplace: an awareness that managers, like all other employees, are fallible human beings attempting to make sense of a rapidly changing planet. An important part of this is linking personal and organizational goals. Organizations are run by people for people. They exist to provide services, goods, and profits. We re-create ourselves through organizations. As a result they reflect our well-being, and they reflect our dis-ease. Bad organizational choices like short-term thinking or desecrating the environment reflect the state of mind of the people who work there. So do smart choices like honoring customers and valuing diversity. Strategies and goals flow from the organization's mission, which, again, is shaped by human motives.

Smart managers help their employees to explore how their personal goals, values, dreams, behaviors, and choices fit into or are supported by the organization's values and goals. This is particularly important as the organizational contract of security and codependence is renegotiated, for downsizing and restructuring create a perceived clash between organizational and personal goals. If this is not managed well, workers become demoralized and there is a draining of the human energy that fuels the organization. To be successful, the organization and its members must become allies focused on caring about customer needs.

## Move from Win-Lose to Win-Win

Many current economic and workplace woes stem from our preoccupation with winners and losers and with the belief that for one person to get his needs met another must lose. Unfortunately, during any crisis or transformational change, it is often easier to adopt a take-it-or-leave-it stance, resulting in situations in which the most powerful always wins. Such has been the case with the less successful attempts to heal and revitalize organizations after downsizing.

To promote healing managers must remember that the best negotiators are those who recognize the possibility of making the pie bigger so that both parties can win. This requires a willingness to explore multiple options, value diversity, listen to understand underlying needs, and work collaboratively to reach creative solutions in which personal goals and organizational goals can be met simultaneously.

## Be Courageous but Flexible

Many managers throw good money after bad either because they go against their better judgment or because they take a position, get feedback from customers and others that it is a bad idea, and dig in to save face. To be trustworthy requires both the courage of conviction and the willingness to adapt when the data requires modifying one's stance. The fear that traps many managers is that, if they stand up for what they believe, they may be publicly proven wrong or that, if they change their minds, they may be seen as weak or wishy-washy. This fear can become a self-fulfilling prophecy in which the very thing a person dreads becomes reality.

By failing to take a stand, we lose our credibility. By refusing to move our stake once we have planted it in the ground, we persist down the wrong path to inevitable failure. Followers ultimately come to respect a leader who has clear values and direction and who is also man or woman enough to listen to feedback, admit mistakes, and correct them.

## Build Trust by Embracing Truth

Parking lot meetings are commonplace in recently downsized organizations. This is a sure sign of the absence of trust. In such meetings people talk about the ideas and feelings they should have raised, but were afraid to, in the real staff meetings. Fearing the repercussions of telling the truth, employees walk on eggshells during the real meeting, and then in a parking lot meeting afterward they talk about, rather than with, their coworkers and bosses. This can be costly in a cost-conscious environment, since good ideas fail to surface and employees' needs, observations, and valuable perspectives are missing from the day-to-day decision-making processes. It is the manager's task to create a work climate in which it is safe — indeed rewarded — to bring all viewpoints to the table.

To pave the way for employees to tell the truth, the manager must model truth telling in his or her own behavior. In his book *Truth & Trust: The First Two Victims of Downsizing*, Frank J. Navran reminds us that "There are no exceptions, no justifications and no rationalizations which suffice to deviate from the position that employees are always entitled to the truth. The fundamental basis of trust in an organization is truth telling. You [the manager] are your employees' best source for honest, accurate, and timely information. The truth is the first essential building block, the foundation, of a trust-based working relationship."

Unfortunately, truth telling does not always occur during organizational transitions. It's not that managers willfully set out to lie. It's simply that they often fear the consequences of telling the whole truth. Concerns about low morale, rumor mill distortions, and whether employees really need to know every detail in order to be effective often become the rationale for withholding the full truth. Another factor is the manager's own denial. I have observed that managers, like other survivors, are sometimes out of touch with the full scope of the realities they face. As mentioned earlier, denial is a natural part of the grieving process. It may well be a useful survival mechanism that blocks us from appreciating the full scope of our losses so that we can continue to cope with day-to-day demands. Unfortunately, if not resolved, this denial can lead to the perception of mistruths and ultimately erode much needed trust between employee and employer. Interestingly, employees surmise the true conditions anyway, especially when they observe that promised increases in operating profits do not readily follow downsizing. In such cases their lowered morale and lost trust is fed by their observation that not all the facts are being shared.

Companies like Westinghouse Electric Corporation now offer a "reality" course to help their downsizing survivors cope with the truth of their emerging workplace. In these sessions the supervisor says point-blank, "It's over; there is no more security. Even though you've survived, there is no guarantee that you'll have a job tomorrow." The response is incredible, the opposite of what one would expect. Survivors heave a collective sigh of relief. Their response is Thanks for having the integrity to finally admit what we knew all along. The most important activity for managers is that of educating workers about the new reality and renegotiating the employee/employer contract so that it more accurately reflects current realities.

## Be Honest Yet Hopeful

I am often challenged by my clients when I tell them to be honest about the present and positive about the future. They tell me that this represents an inherent contradiction. They quiet down, however, after I point out that the real contradiction is being in a managerial position, charged with leadership—taking people to a better place—and not believing that it is possible. Yet, there are many burned-out bosses in downsizing organizations whose morale is low and who tell their employees, "It's going to be hell, but follow me." It is important to paint an accurate picture of the challenges current and future. It is important to talk about what is changing and why, as well as what will remain the same. In this regard it is useful to engage employees in assessing what does work well. The manager's goal is to get people to disengage from the past, not obliterate it. The lessons of past experience can be invaluable in the process of change. In fact, as part of a downsizing and restructuring process, many good companies find their equilibrium by returning to their core businesses—doing the things they are really good at, even better than before.

In leading a transition to the future, it is equally important to paint an exciting vision of where the organization needs to go or what it could become. Only then can the manager-leader hope to support survivors in letting go of the familiar security to take creative leaps into the unknown. Only then can he or she enlist and align people behind the vision, bringing all of their talents and other resources to bear on creating a new beginning.

### Become an Expert in Cultural Change

Everyone agrees that we need to fundamentally change the way we do business, the way we conceptualize work, and the way we relate to one another as employer, employee, customer, supplier, or investor. To be successful, survivor managers must become experts in cultural change. This begins with the ability to heal the emotional wounds inflicted by loss and the feelings of insecurity associated with any transition. It also involves dealing with inertia. It is an interesting paradox that Humex's customers perceived that the company was not changing fast enough to meet their escalating needs for value and quality, while Humex's employees complained that "there are too many changes." Ironically, organization members tend to re-create what is familiar, even as they face the need to change in order to survive.

Rosabeth Moss Kanter has contributed much to our understanding of why people resist change. Her research has revealed a number of reasons, including a loss of control, fear of the unknown, the need to save face, the fact that change means more work initially, and the fact that it means a temporary loss of competence as people adjust. Kanter also reminds us that people resist change because "sometimes the threat is real." In the case of workers, changing their codependent relationship to one of independence can mean a threat to their jobs, but as we know, this fear is pointless, since their jobs are already threatened.

When change does occur, as it eventually must if we are not to die, we move through three distinct phases. Like the trapeze artist, we start out by holding on to the swing in a momentary comfort, or safety, zone. As discussed earlier, denial and a refusal to move forward are part of this holding-on stage in organizational life. Then comes the awful, awe-filled moment of letting go and plunging into the nothingness of William Bridges's neutral zone, which greets the trapeze artist in between the time she lets go of one swing and grabs hold of the next. The audience holds its breath in this moment, which holds the possibility of certain death in the absence of a safety net. But it also holds the possibility of a creative rebirth. If the trapeze artist succeeds, she grabs hold of the second swing, embracing the new.

These phases are often described in the context of organizational cultural change as unfreezing, moving, and refreezing. In leading organizational change, managers must develop the expertise to create conditions that move people from holding on to the old ways of thinking and doing things to the necessary letting go (unfreezing), in which they move through fear, uncertainty, confusion, and anxiety in the direction of change (moving). Finally, the manager must provide the incentives, resources, and plan of action that make it possible for downsizing survivors to embrace the new realities (refreezing) and begin the process of learning to exist in a new state until further change is warranted.

## Provide Resources and Support

Doing more with less has turned out to be the organizational myth of the eighties and nineties. It is possible to do more with less up to a point, especially if the organization was, in fact, too fat for its own good. And that is often the case. Most organizations, however, have gone to a point of diminishing returns. They need to address resource management and consider the possibility that they may need more in the way of training, time, technology, creativity, technical support, and other resources to do more. Retooling to keep pace with technology and growing competition is important for survival. Trimming costs and budgets in a way that is not mindful of this requirement can lead to obsolescence.

People need individual reassurances that they are valued and that they will get the support they need to succeed in a changing environment. One of my colleagues, a former manager at Mellon Bank, shared the story of how her manager took each member of his staff aside following layoffs and explained to each one how they were valuable to the organization, what skills they needed to develop to continue to succeed, and what new performance goals they needed to concentrate on. "It was very comforting to me," she said, "because it answered the most important question—the question that was threatening to block my performance: How come I wasn't laid off?" She went on to add that, following the personal session, she experienced renewed energy and a renewed commitment to her organization.

### Provide Training and Lifelong Learning Opportunities

Training involves many simultaneous activities. The first set of activities involves the development of managerial and leadership skills. The conditions spawned by mergers, acquisitions, layoffs, and reengineering require a new set of skills. In this climate managers must be clear about their own values and direction and particularly about the "value-added competence" they bring to the act of transforming organizations. That is, beyond the routine expectations of their assigned business roles, managers must bring fresh insights and new perspectives to their positions. Self-reflection and self-mastery are key prerequisites. The popularity of 360° leadership assessment tools attests to a growing awareness that feedback from others is necessary for managers to identify their strengths and areas for improvement as they lead change.

Managers must also be comfortable with ambiguity and rapid change. They must negotiate the many paradoxes of leadership nineties style. These include dilemmas such as inspiring often demoralized workers to innovate, while making drastic cuts, or getting more work better, faster, and with fewer resources. Specifically, managers must cultivate leadership and coaching skills aimed at inspiring and managing change as they build trust and create high-performing interdisciplinary teams. They must understand the role and benefits of valuing and managing diverse perspectives and needs in an increasingly multicultural environment. They must then develop techniques for managing differences, resolving conflicts, and negotiating win-win outcomes both internally and externally.

The second set of activities promotes lifelong learning and flexible thinking as core competencies for all employees on an equal par with other strategic business and organizational competencies.

As we seek a better life socially, economically, and spiritually, we must remember that work is part of the natural rhythm of human explorations. Our "handiwork" is an extension of our thoughts, our talents, our capabilities. We measure our competence and our self-worth by our ability to be effective (i.e., to achieve results) as a parent, a carpenter, an engineer, a teacher, a manager, a waiter, a griot, an artist, or a governor. As discussed earlier, people who are most fulfilled are those who effectively develop the skills to blend these various aspects of their lives.

*Encourage a Movement from Surviving to Thriving*

Getting people to do what's needed is different from getting them to feel good about it. The difference between surviving and thriving after downsizing can be measured by whether workers remain in a compliance mode (doing what they are told because "this is just a job") or move to commitment (caring and investing fully in the new direction). The chart below provides a summary of the change in stance necessary for people to move from merely surviving to thriving.

| FROM COMPLIANCE (surviving) | TO COMMITMENT (thriving) |
| --- | --- |
| going along with | enrolling in |
| doing | wanting to do |
| conforming | supporting |
| obeying | collaborating |
| following | coleading |
| reacting | cocreating |
| dependence | interdependence |
| powerless | empowered |

### *Become Comfortable with Being Uncomfortable*

An important first step on the journey toward healing the downsized organization is to get everyone to be comfortable with being uncomfortable. The new workplace reality is that we can no longer exist in a comfort zone regarding job security or an organization's future. Things are changing rapidly, and the ability to anticipate, embrace, and manage change in oneself and in the organization are the keys to reduced stress and an improved quality of work life. In the success stories that follow in later chapters, I will provide examples of how some organizations are successfully imparting this new philosophy.

### *Set Outrageous Goals*

Corporate and government leaders insist that they are engaged in transformational change, but often they make only minor transitional shifts. Some remain caught in the trap of doing the same program and process changes over and over, with interesting, and sometimes even effective, evolutionary variations and improvements each time. To mark the changes, they ritualistically rename each initiative but keep doing the same sorts of things. If you keep on doing what you've always done, you'll keep on getting what you've always gotten.

In planning for change, the manager must communicate in no uncertain terms that things will never be the same. This includes a well-crafted, engaging vision of the desired outcomes, along with specific goals and milestones. Bold steps must then be taken to engage all people in the process—moving beyond mere compliance (doing what they are told) to commitment (embracing the process as their own). In short, to achieve breakthrough innovations, the manager must set outrageous goals and get people to exceed them.

## CREATING A HEALING ENVIRONMENT

As we reinvent government, reengineer businesses, reform education, and redesign not-for-profit organizations, the manager's effectiveness hinges on his or her ability to create, and re-create when necessary, a workplace culture that heals losses and sustains performance. Managers must reinvent workplaces to equip employees to accommodate a new breed of demanding customers, compete in a world economy, develop the skills and talents to perform effectively, and simultaneously battle a host of new social and business challenges. Systematic efforts must be instituted in the aftermath of downsizing and restructuring to re-create the workplace to achieve these goals. Few managers have the skills to do this well.

The most difficult hurdle for survivors is letting go of their old expectations of the employee/employer relationship. The most difficult hurdle for survivor managers is creating the healing conditions to support and embrace change.

In healing the downsized organization, managers must balance their focus on creating and eliminating jobs to include a focus on rehabilitating the workplace. As part of the preparation of workers for the emerging workplace, the selection of new employees and the retooling of existing ones must center on preserving the workers' self-esteem. This self-esteem is rendered fragile by the breakup, shrinking, merging, restructuring, and reengineering of businesses and other organizations, leaving employees to reorient and redefine themselves and their place in the scheme of things. This is a major challenge for even the most seasoned manager. It is also a wonderful opportunity to start over again from scratch—to play a central role in creating the workplace of the future as we move out of the industrial age into the first wave of the information age. It is a chance to create new processes and practices and a truly motivating work climate. But first the healing must take place after the wounds of transformational change have taken their toll.

In the chapters that follow we will look at the successes of several organizations that embarked on similar journeys. Each encountered a reduction in its workforce. Each confronted the task of reinventing the organization and rebuilding momentum so as to be positioned more competitively for the future. The stories are encouraging because they remind us that it is possible for employees and managers to face the inevitable losses associated with change and to collaborate successfully in healing themselves and their organizations as they rethink and redesign processes and practices to remain competitive.

## SURVIVOR MANAGER CLOSE-UP

Denny Ross is a long-term Westinghouse employee. He worked his way through various jobs from engineer to manager of quality in the company's Nuclear Services Division. Like employees everywhere these days, he has had to deal with anxieties about the future. As a concerned manager, his sense of responsibility in a downsizing, restructuring business unit extends beyond his own future. In Ross's words: "When technicians go home, they worry about themselves and their families.

When I go home, I worry about myself and my subordinates and their families."

When the then division manager, Tom Christopher, asked Ross to join his team in 1991, morale was on the decline, as was business performance. The division was making money, but operating profits as a percentage of sales were very low. Ross's charge was to lead a total quality management effort as a driving force to revitalize the business and employees' spirits.

Ross's approach was to take the best practices within the Westinghouse nuclear business as the benchmarks. The Commercial Nuclear Fuel Division (CNFD) was a good role model. It had won the Malcolm Baldrige Quality Award a few years earlier, and it had in place a process for establishing operations measures against which everyone performed. CNFD had also instituted an effective leadership course that played a critical role in empowering managers and technical professionals to think "outside the box" and to develop skills for shared decision making, and team building.

Working closely with Allen Burnett, the organizational development and leadership training specialist on his staff, Ross also reviewed the best training programs available outside the company to support both NSD senior staff and employees in managing their way through the challenges of downsizing and restructuring the business. Among their critical interventions was development of a business performance improvement plan (BPIP) that helped the division define its direction and, through a series of key issues, determine how it intended to get there. They then instituted leadership training and team building for the senior staff and for all managers and professionals in the department. Ross says,

> The leadership training was a major strategy for helping employees deal with their morale issues and their insecurity about the future. It provided a forum through which people could share their frustrations, and get support from their colleagues in moving forward. It also taught them an important lesson that should prepare them well for the future: you don't have to be a

manager to help lead your company out of a crisis. Everyone is being helped through the course to embrace the idea of shared leadership and of self-directed work teams. After three days in this support group kind of setting, most employees left the leadership course feeling more empowered.

Another important aspect of the leadership course instituted by Ross was that the division manager visited every session and held a sort of town meeting in which employees could voice their concerns, ask tough questions, and get straight, honest answers. This worked so well that it planted the seed for the next managerial intervention that Ross and Burnett implemented: the "Reality '95" course.

As part of their initiatives to develop leadership, they had reviewed and adopted for senior management the *Fortune* magazine seminar developed by Noel Tichy called "Mastering Revolutionary Change." This course planted the seed for an important intervention with employees. It gave management the courage and the skills to face the hard business realities jointly with employees. Ross says,

> In the past the company line had been "these are hard times, but they'll get better, just hang in and work smarter." Employees questioned the pep talks, and they gave us feedback that they just didn't buy it. We came to realize that we need to give employees credit for their ability to handle tough news. We had learned from the "Mastering Revolutionary Change" course that you can use tough news to create a sense of urgency.
>
> So I launched "Reality '95" at NSD. We got our training folks to put together an informational program in which we looked at our customers, our business environment, our company, and our workforce. We gathered data and figures on the state of things like deregulation in the utilities industry and the effect of the resulting competition on our future. Every manager had to learn these business realities and teach them to their employees with support from an internal trainer. We also linked this information to the BPIP. This frank, factual education became a turning point in restoring some degree of trust

and employee involvement. While they still shared the anxieties of layoff survivors everywhere, they felt we have come clean and we were approaching them as true partners in the problem-solving and decision-making process.

Teaching the "Reality '95" course was a pivotal event for Ross. As a manager, he felt that it worked on several levels. It engaged the senior staff in learning more about the change process and how to support and manage employees through that process. It also enabled them to clarify their own direction and goals. By engaging managers in teaching their employees about the business realities that managers struggle with, it allowed for much-needed team building, and it has created an environment in which the message is consistent. Ross believes that

> "Reality '95" has led to an understanding on the part of the workforce of the Westinghouse business challenges and the necessary changes for our survival in the utilities industry. But the most important outcome has been to help us begin to let go of the old expectations and move into the zone of readiness for change. Employees can handle the reality of the situation if we just involve them and allow them to become partners in working through our crises.

# *Part II*

—∾—

# THE SEARCH
# FOR HEALTHY
# PRACTICES

# INTRODUCTION

Viewed from employees' perspective, a healthy organization is one in which people are generally satisfied with the quality of their work life. On most days they feel good about going to work. They feel empowered to help shape decisions that affect them, they have the resources and skills to satisfy customer needs, and they are generally confident in the abilities of the organization's leadership team. From the organization's perspective, the organization is healthy if it is viable as measured by its profitability, competitive market position, and customer satisfaction. A healthy organization also responds well to the need for change; it is adaptive and thereby ensures its future survival. This means that following a major upheaval or transition the healthy organization rebounds. It does not remain in a state of chaos and pain, but rather finds the degree of equilibrium needed to continue to succeed.

This is the definition of "healing" that informed my search for success stories for this book. To gauge the overall well-being of each downsized organization I visited, I administered a written survey and held focus group interviews with management and nonmanagement employees. My goal was to note their feelings and opinions about the organization and its management as the organization worked its way back from the trauma of downsizing toward relative wholeness.

I unwittingly created discomfort in several organizations by posing the question "Was your downsizing successful from the point of view of the survivors?" In a couple of organizations, my query caused different managerial factions to argue about whether what they had on their hands was a "success." Many managers claimed to have had great success, but their employees disagreed adamantly. The greatest surprise for me during the writing of this book was the fact that very few managers had thought about or planned for survivor needs during the process. They launched their downsizing and restructuring initiatives guided by criteria for successful outplacement, successful cost reduction, and successful profitability gains, but not for addressing the concerns of those who would be charged with making the changes happen. One Fortune 500 company executive confided, "We have been downsizing for years, since 1980, [and] we have never asked the survivors how they felt about it. I guess we're sort of afraid to know!"

The downsized organizations that I have chosen to present in this section from among the many I interviewed are offered as examples of lessons learned and, in some cases, as best practices. These organizations do not claim to be perfect, nor are they without shortcomings. What distinguishes them, however, is that they went about downsizing and restructuring in a manner that was mindful of the impact on survivors as they planned for change and after the change was initiated.

Along the way I learned that organizational healing occurs largely because of individual choices made by managers and other employees about how they will manage themselves and how they will lead others. Some individuals stood out as exemplary "healers" based on the personal choices they made for managing themselves and interfacing with the organization. In addition to the organizational profiles, I have provided cameo portraits of several of these healers.

The leaders and managers in each organization combined the need to take invasive measures, such as cutting employees, eliminating businesses, outsourcing services, and increasing workloads, with procedures to ensure healing and the future well-being of the organization and its survivors. In doing so, each organization knowingly or unwittingly created a healing community marked by positive survivor perceptions of four important "postoperative" conditions: fairness, honesty, legitimacy, and viability. These conditions have been carefully documented in studies on downsizing over a ten-year period as holding the key to whether survivors respond positively or negatively in the long run. In essence, employees' views about how the changes were executed and whether management did the right thing are key determinants of the survivor experience. As discussed in chapter 2, these beliefs also shape the employees' stance toward the organization and their willingness to participate fully in reinventing the organization.

In my survey of survivors, I categorized their reactions to downsizing under four headings: perceptions, personal feelings and stance, individual impact and behavior, and impact on the organization.

## PERCEPTIONS

We observed that the downsizing survivor initially forms perceptions about the event along four important dimensions: the fairness, honesty, and legitimacy in handling the layoff victims and survivors and the viability of the business afterward.

### Fairness

In the successful organizations we studied, employees perceived that those who left and they, as survivors, were treated fairly. Typically, their self-reported criteria for fairness included a generous severance package and assistance with outplacement for those who left and increased compensation and/or other resources, such as training and technology, for those who remained.

*Honesty*

On this dimension employees' perception of the integrity of the leadership was shaped primarily by four variables:

- the degree and quality of prior communication about driving forces and plans for change;
- the willingness of management to share accurate information about such matters as past mistakes and current realities;
- clear directives from management regarding expectations for the company's future and especially for each employee's role in that future;
- the degree of truthfulness demonstrated by senior management, measured by the consistency between what management promised and what actually occurred during and after the changes.

*Legitimacy*

Employees who perceive legitimate business reasons for downsizing and restructuring are more likely to embrace these changes in the long run, even if they initially resist or are negatively impacted by them. In each success story employees agreed that their organizations had no choice but to change in order to survive. Furthermore, through effective communication, or "a healthy dose of reality" as one manager put it, these employees fully understood the external and internal driving forces for change. In each case employees held the perception that the decisions were tied to future opportunities and to the organization's mission and distinctive competence, as well as to present challenges, and not just to "numbers" and "reducing head count."

*Viability*

The perception of viability was measured by whether surviving employees felt moderately secure to very secure about the future. In each case employees expressed the belief that the organization was now better positioned than before to carry forward its mission, compete effectively, and satisfy customer needs. In each organization viability was also demonstrated by objective measures such as company profits, return on equity, increased market share, and so forth.

These survivor judgments about whether or not downsizing was handled fairly, whether or not management was honest, whether or not it was a smart business decision, and whether the organization was now more or less viable than before determined the survivors' emotional response as measured by feelings about the changes and their stance toward the organization.

## PERSONAL FEELINGS AND STANCE

Members of an organization bring to it all of their longings and their beliefs about work, about authority, about success. They also bring their past experiences and their unfinished psychological business to the work world. In corporate meetings, if we observe carefully, we can peer through the veneer of businesslike certainty to discover along with it unresolved childhood issues, like the fear of separation, the need for approval, or the desire for security. At some level there is an unspoken expectation that these needs ought to be met by the organizations that hire us.

Similarly, the organization holds its own set of expectations for us. As John Sculley, former CEO of Apple Computer, once put it, the new corporate contract asks workers to leash themselves to the corporate dream, at least for a while. In leashing ourselves to the organization's dream, our feelings about the organization are formed at the juncture where our personal dreams and the organization's intersect. If both dreams collide in a clash of competing interests, the employee adopts a negative stance. If both are compatible, the employee tends to feel more positive toward the organization. The attitudes and feelings listed above then become barometers of employee satisfaction and organizational well-being.

In assessing survivors' personal feelings and stance toward the organization, I used a written survey as well as interview questions to gauge the level of the following:

- trust (directed toward senior management);
- empowerment in the decision-making and problem-solving processes;
- security;
- stress;
- hopefulness about the organization's future;
- turnover intent;
- job satisfaction.

## INDIVIDUAL IMPACT AND BEHAVIOR

Consciously or subconsciously the behaviors survivors chose were direct reflections of the feelings and stances described above. In assessing the impact on individuals, we looked for evidence of the following:

- commitment;
- willingness to take risks;
- creativity;
- performance;
- productivity;
- perceived availability of resources to do one's job.

## IMPACT ON THE ORGANIZATION

The above perceptions, feelings and stance, and behaviors have multiple and ripple effects. Taken together, they shape the climate of the organization. The workplace may be energized or drained; workers may be observed to have high morale or low morale. Worker stress, marked by high absenteeism, lowered creativity, and lessened productivity, ultimately shows up as organizational performance issues. As a result of these behavioral responses to the survivors' perceptions and feelings, the organization will ultimately be more or less profitable, be more or less competitive, and achieve more or less customer satisfaction.

We measured the organizational impact by the members' conclusion about three factors:

- profitability and financial viability;
- competitive position in the marketplace;
- customer satisfaction.

# Chapter 4

—m—

# THE COPPERWELD CASE

"In real simple terms it is like cutting down this big, unwieldy bush that was scraggly, not growing very well, not very healthy. You cut it down close to the ground, close to its healthy base, and then what happens? It comes back up and flourishes with new growth." These words of Copperweld president and CEO John Turner capture the spirit and the intent of the company's decision to downsize and restructure itself in the mid-1980s. Yet, Turner is quick to add, "It was very traumatic, troubling because we were dealing with people's lives, and as a senior manager my responsibility is . . . to make sure that we have a viable company that can provide the security for as many people as possible. [Yet] I can't have a successful company and provide security for more people than the business will support. And that's why the restructuring had to take place."

Like thousands of mature companies in today's manufacturing industry, Copperweld, the world's largest producer of bimetallic wire products and a leader in the tubing industry, was challenged by global competition and shrinking markets at the same time that it faced the possibility of buckling under its own weight. As one employee put it, "The company had been fat and happy for too long." The reality of an economy in which the metal industry was hurting and in which Copperweld's steel bar operations were no longer profitable forced the company to eliminate redundancies and refocus itself in order to survive. The company's strategy was to spin off its steel bar operations at CSC Industries, revitalize its core businesses—bimetallics and tubing—launch a seven-year modernization program in its wire and tubing plants, and through acquisitions grow the company in a very focused way.

This strategy was accompanied by a series of dramatic and necessary changes in the structure and composition of the workforce. First, there were several moves over a one-year period to consolidate production facilities geographically so that similar products were housed in a single facility. During this process corporate staff members, information systems personnel, and employees from marketing and sales were centrally relocated to the Pittsburgh office. This move highlighted several glaring redundancies in staffing. There were too many managers and too many layers of management. In an unprecedented move, Copperweld downsized its senior management staff in one day by over 60 percent. This meant going from thirteen corporate officers to three and from a corporate staff of sixty people to twenty-two, thus creating a flatter organization. In addition, a new, and philosophically very different, leadership team was installed after the downsizing was completed, sending a clear message that the organization was in the process of transforming itself.

The remaining workforce was downsized and restructured as well. The company's Data Center was outsourced to Genix, but exemplary measures were taken to minimize the job losses. Three employees in the Data Center were hired by Genix, for example, and all were offered a bonus to remain through the end of the year-long restructuring. In the various divisions approximately 20 percent of all salaried jobs were lost.

The net effect of this transformation was the creation of a new culture to replace the old. At the visible level of this new culture, it was evident that the structure of the organization, its composition, work practices, and methods of reward were all significantly different.

At the less visible level of Copperweld's culture there were perceptible shifts in values and expectations reported by everyone we interviewed. Copperweld had transformed itself from an overstaffed, inefficient, political, top-down bureaucracy into a lean, flexible, team-oriented, customer-driven organization. In describing the old culture employees reflected on the fact that things used to be more adversarial, with "lots of competing egos" and personality conflicts. The old culture was excessive, marked by redundancies in roles, and focused on growth for remuneration. The new culture, in contrast, was efficient. There were fewer layers, and certain functions, such as information systems, had been outsourced to a vendor who could do the job in a more cost-effective manner. This freed up the company to concentrate on what it did best.

In contrast to the old command-and-control approach, the leadership in the new culture was described by everyone as more accessible and more willing to communicate openly in a two-way manner. Information was shared regularly from the top, and input was sought, and listened to, from employees at every level.

Copperweld's headquarters at Four Gateway Center epitomizes Pittsburgh, a city transforming itself from smokestacks to high tech, from hierarchical silos to matrixed teams. Leaving the elevators on the twenty-second floor, we lowered our voices as we entered Copperweld's sedate, tastefully appointed executive offices. After cordial greetings and gracious hospitality, we were ushered in to meet John Turner.

In many respects Turner and his senior management team are not unlike the organization man of the fifties. They are essentially white, middle-class, family-centered men who are dedicated to building a secure future for their company and themselves. But they are different because they are also men of the nineties.

As nineties managers they know the reality of a workplace that can make few promises about job security. "We didn't promise there would be no more layoffs," says Eugene Pocci, vice president of human resources; "we said there were no plans for further layoffs at this point in time. There is a big distinction. Today we need to understand that conditions of success or failure, profit or loss, determine the future. How we satisfy the customer determines our future security. We should infer that if the company is successful we will be part of that. If it is not successful, obviously the other side of the coin will surface."

As nineties managers, members of the senior staff of Copperweld have lived through at least one major downsizing in which their own jobs were possible targets, and they have experienced the anxiety and shock of survivor status. Here is how one survivor manager described his brush with the radical termination of management jobs in 1985:

> I could see it coming down the hall. I was walking down the hall, and I could see someone at the other end of the hall leaving. People—managers—were leaving their office with their jackets slung over their shoulders at ten in the morning. You knew what was happening. But it was fast. I don't know how many designated executioners they had, but they just started circulating around the office, going into each individual's office, and it almost had the appearance that it was done at one time, but it could not possibly have been done at one time with so many people.

A colleague nodded, affirming the trauma of the situation, and added, "There is no good way to do something like that. It is painful."

So how does a company like Copperweld, like so many other manufacturing organizations today, move past the shock and the pain of such massive cost-cutting operations to begin the process of healing and to create an even better organism in its wake?

The Copperweld managers I interviewed are externally focused, skilled at reading customer needs and at scanning the global environment with a proactive stance, ready to make strategic choices to ensure their future viability. Yet they are equally focused internally on their surviving employees' well-being. They are interested in dialogue with employees at all levels. In fact, Turner and his staff go to great lengths to demonstrate that they view all employees as an integral part of the Copperweld team. As a part of restructuring, there are at present only four layers between the CEO and the frontline plant employees, compared to a previous chain of command that was seven layers deep. There are fewer employees generating a greater percentage of the work and the profits for the company. The time clocks have been removed from the shop floor, and Turner makes monthly visits to each Copperweld plant in order to meet with every employee in small groups over breakfast, lunch, or dinner. In these meetings he holds informal two-way dialogues and attempts to answer all questions directly and honestly. Compensation is now based on profitability. Through a profit-sharing plan, employees reap generous bonuses based on their team's performance. This means that rewarding employees is tied to an increasingly team-oriented and customer-centered way of doing business. The new philosophy is reminiscent of that of Jack Welch, CEO of General Electric, who once said that "companies can't grant security, only customers can."

Team effectiveness is also central to the emerging Copperweld culture. While the company has individual performance appraisals, they are tied more to employee feedback and development. Compensation is based on team performance. If the team does well, everyone at the plant and at the corporate level benefits.

## LESSONS FROM COPPERWELD

The story of Copperweld's revitalization offers many lessons. In our interviews managers and employees at various levels unanimously agreed on the following.

## Stick to What You Do Best

Copperweld's success lies largely in its return to its core businesses—bimetallics and tubing. Over the years the company has consistently responded to and, more importantly, anticipated what its customers need. Rather than going the route of many big businesses that follow trends, Copperweld's strategy has been to seek "the right thing" for the customer. This is not to say that the company does not keep abreast of changes or that it has not gained acceptance and recognition for important leading-edge management trends. Copperweld is, like many companies in its business league, ISO certified. It has a Q1 (Quality 1) rating, which is the highest automotive industry qualification, at Ford. The company also has achieved recognition from its other automotive clients, including Targets of Excellence awards from General Motors and the Quality Seal of Approval from Chrysler. All of this speaks to the focus on excellence in customer service that is based on the propensity to do what the company does best. One key result of this is that employees are focused and unified behind a clear vision of what the company stands for. When a company restructures, this is a critical ingredient in rallying the surviving forces.

## Cut Quickly and Deeply, and Do It Once

Employees and managers alike at the Copperweld offices in Pittsburgh can still recall the shock and the pain on the fateful morning in the mid-1980s when manager after manager left the corporate headquarters for good. As is always the case with these events, they experienced feelings of loss, denial, and insecurity—wondering whether at any moment they, too, would be called in for their walking papers—and the relief, mixed with guilt, when they survived the cuts.

This is how a group of middle managers recalled their feelings. "After the cuts, people were stunned. We all just walked around dazed. It did not just end in one day. . . . Those let go were people we knew. They were our friends. It wasn't just the senior level. We had known them for some time. We were concerned about them; what were they going to do?"

"Yet it certainly helped that it was such a busy time, because so many people had left. There were so many pieces to pick up. You really were occupied."

"That certainly helped."

"With me there certainly was a feeling of depression. I was grieving for the friends that I knew. But I guess it is sort of a surprising reaction because as a survivor you should think, 'Wow! I really dodged a bullet there! I'm sitting pretty now and everything looks rosy for me.' And yet I felt really bad."

"Well, with me it was 'Gee, what did I do right?' Or, 'That could have been me.' Or, 'Why am I so lucky?' Guilt."

"You feel bad because you were lucky."

"I was packing. [I figured] they are going from the top down. Then Doug came in and said, 'You aren't leaving. Put your shoes back on!' "

Yet all agree that the way the company managed downsizing was humane. It was done swiftly and completely so that people could begin their grieving and their healing. According to Turner,

> We needed to get on with it so that we could deal with those affected in a very humane way, in a very compassionate way. What we did was, we said there were going to be some people who would be out of work as a result of the changes. But whatever our policy for layoffs has been, we are going to do considerably more than that as far as financial considerations are concerned, and we are going to work with all of them in outplacement for as long as it takes. We didn't put a deadline on it. The wording was "until satisfactory employment was found." And we didn't put a dollar figure on it because our greater concern was the human element.

> Fortunately, since that period there have been very few instances where we have had to lay off any people. We don't want to do that. What we do is we'll work overtime, we'll work six

and seven days a week. We'll do everything we can in order that in the good times we are providing significant overtime opportunities so when the business slacks off the overtime goes down, but the jobs don't go away. Now, there's no guarantee we can always do that in any set of economic situations. But we have been very successful at that in the past. We really want to avoid layoffs whenever possible.

The employees I spoke with held the same opinion:

From other stories that I've heard it seems like the swift and sure method is the best. One company I know . . . came out and had big meetings with people and said, "Hey, somewhere down the line we are going to fire a whole bunch of people. We don't know who yet, or when. Now go back and do your job." [From then on] it was like working in a morgue from what I understand. To me that is the exact opposite of the way it should be handled. It sounds cruel, but we were swift, and I think it was better for all parties concerned in the long run. To wander around and not know would be even tougher. You sort of get on with your life. And I'm sure it is the case with even those laid off. Some people took it fairly well, recognizing they were let go, while others were very bitter . . . [but they knew immediately what their fate was and could move on].

## Be Honest and Compassionate

By all accounts one critical event was senior management's decision to call the surviving employees into a meeting at which they were given assurances about a number of things, including the following:

- an explanation of what was done and why;
- assurances that there were no further changes or layoffs planned;
- a discussion of the new jobs and new relationships;
- an affirmation of their importance to the company and its future;

- acknowledgment that the workload would increase but that there would be grace demonstrated if employees were unable to accomplish everything before them. As a means of coping with the added demands on their time, they were encouraged to focus on high-priority items first and worry less about low-priority items.

Following this all-employee meeting at the William Penn Hotel, department managers then followed up by consistently reinforcing the above messages with their own staffs as a group and individually. Engaging employees this way empowered them, through information sharing and joint problem solving, to embrace their role in the renewing company.

"People's jobs were so dramatically different, or [involved] so much more quantitywise. . . . We would meet basically every day as a department just to communicate and support each other. Every day we got into a meeting room and said, 'Okay, what is the problem today?' We did that I bet for a month. And that was really helpful because people really had a forum. We could go and get help if we were stumped or really feeling exasperated or whatever."

"Yeah, we did a lot of communicating, even with the people in Brazil. We did a lot of having people express themselves, their concerns."

"While it was pretty unsettling, the communication helped. My new boss came shortly after the layoffs and talked to all of us at the same time in a department meeting. Pretty much he went over what was done, who was no longer with the company, the reasons—mainly cutting costs. He thought we couldn't move forward as an organization like we had in the past. He realized we all had new jobs and tough jobs. But he urged us to just get down and do it. We started doing it that minute."

"Yes, and we were given assurances that there are fewer people to do the same job now, so don't be overly concerned if things fall between the cracks. There was the assurance that it will take us a while to figure out what things were simply unnecessary pieces of work that were not to be done anymore, and there is no sense in wringing our hands over trying to do everything that was done before."

## *Let Survivors Know That They are Valued and Valuable*

Interestingly, one of the most successful strategies following Copperweld's downsizing was the fact that managers repeatedly assured employees that they were valued by, and valuable to, the company. Some employees told us that they were left with the feeling that they were survivors because they were special to the company in some important way. The fact that Copperweld's management position was clearly "do your best—we recognize you may not be able to accomplish everything, but that's okay as long as you focus on priorities" went a long way toward keeping employees positive and motivated as they dealt with the increasing workload and the losses of restructuring.

In Turner's words, "I don't think you can overemphasize enough the people aspect of downsizing and restructuring. There is not only responsibility here for 1,300 people, there is responsibility for 1,300 people's families; you can't ever lose sight of that fact . . . and then they touch a number of people. So that's why the responsibility is to continue to provide a viable company so that we can provide security for those people."

## *Keep People Informed*

"I mean, I'm boring!" says Turner, when he speaks of the messages he repeatedly communicates so that everyone will be clear about the company's vision, direction, and priorities.

> You ask the people. They'll tell you I keep harping on the same thing. I keep talking about the importance of blocking and tackling, doing the mundane things very well, doing them very consistently. You know we talk about customer service, superior performance in the areas of customer service. We talk about leading the focus on our quality position, on productivity

and efficiency, on the basic building blocks of a business and not losing sight, not losing focus on what that is. This is not a high-tech kind of a business; it's basic. You've gotta stick to the basics. . . . We are a very market-driven company. In other words, we take great pains and strides to ensure that we understand what our customers need, in many cases even before they realize they need it, and try to be on the forefront in a proactive way. Everything we do on the business side starts out with "What does the customer need?"

What distinguishes the Copperweld story are the unanimous sentiments of loyalty and admiration directed at CEO John Turner. The comments invariably centered on the clarity and consistency of his message and his leadership. "He sets a clear direction, without telling us exactly what to do," was an observation offered in various ways by managers and nonmanagers alike. "We are clear about priorities, and we get rewarded for working hard and fulfilling those priorities," was another typical comment, demonstrating the positive relationship between goals and payoffs.

Strategically, Turner sees his commitment to clear, redundant communication as giving him an edge in a competitive arena.

Even though Copperweld spent a significant amount of money on capital, other people also have the ability to spend money on capital. Where we distinguish ourselves is in the way we train, communicate, and empower people. Our people know what the vision is. They know what the objectives are. Then [they are given] a great deal of influence in how they do their job. We encourage employee suggestions. We encourage employee involvement so much so that we have all 1,300 people trying to figure out ways to do what they control better.

## To Win Trust, Treat People Fairly

A group of Copperweld middle managers I spoke with categorized Turner and his senior management team as "very approachable and trustworthy." One of the managers explained, "They gained a lot of credibility with us [managers] and the rest of the employee population over the years. . . . They are open. They make it a part of their job to communicate with their employees, both face-to-face and through written communications." Echoing that sentiment, a second manager added, "There is much more communication between VPs and the regular people. In the past the VPs and CEO were inaccessible; now we are all like part of the same company."

When I probed further about how specifically this company spirit was inspired, the comments once again centered on the leadership of CEO Turner. The words used to describe this trusted, charismatic figure included "visionary," "mentally tough," "trustworthy," "walks the talk," "flexible," "honest," "focused," "intelligent," "competent," and "consistent between his rhetoric and behavior." His staff members were equally complimentary: "He is open to challenge and receives feedback well." "He knows what he's doing." "He cares about people. He has our best interests at heart."

When I met with Turner, I decided to ask him about his philosophy and the beliefs that informed his leadership practices, which are legendary among Copperweld employees. Slightly embarrassed by my question, which had gotten away from a discussion of business strategy to things more personal, he gave me the following explanation:

> I think it all falls back to a spirituality of life. I believe that the whole genesis of this business philosophy centers around my overall view of life and my core values. It's not just about work, because in the big scheme of things work is important, but it is not the most important thing. I believe there is no substitute for trust—no way to recapture trust once lost. I can go out there and talk to these people for ten years and be straightforward. But if there is one deed, if there is one misstep, if there is one decision that is made to betray that trust, I'm done or whoever else does it is done. That can't be regained, so you have to take trust and you have to put a little protective shield around it. You

better make sure that you don't violate that. And so trust requires communication so that people don't misconstrue what is being done as a misdeed. And then you have to be very consistent, or you will lose their trust.

## *Put a Positive Spin on Everything*

In talking about his philosophy Turner also added that a positive nature is central to his character and his approach to healing his restructured organization and to leading employees into the future: "Try, try always to put a positive attitude on everything you're doing," he advises, "even the things where you are looking to improve something, where you are looking to recover from some problem you had in the plant, or some problem you had with a customer, or a relationship, or anything. When you are giving criticism, give it in a positive, constructive way. I try to always recognize the good that people have. I try to recognize their need for self-worth and protect their self-esteem."

## *Reward and Celebrate People*

Copperweld today is guided by the belief that everyone should participate in the rewards associated with profitability. The workforce understands that when business is good they reap the benefits of their effective work. Conversely, if the business is less profitable, they are held accountable. This approach of variable compensation goes a long way toward survivor healing because it sends the unambiguous message that employees have ownership in the company. This gives them a sense of security. It is also a key motivational factor. Researchers have consistently demonstrated that employees are more motivated to go the extra mile when they experience a direct cause-and-effect relationship between effort and rewards. This is also key in today's business environment. The old assumption was that employee performance should be tied to promotions up the managerial ladder. The old hierarchical compensation approach is no longer practical as organizations flatten and de-layer their management structure. The Copperweld performance reward system is both relevant for the new competitive global economy and highly motivating for its work teams.

As Turner summed it up,

> It's all about people. You can pat people on the back, you can encourage people for working hard, but it's more important to recognize and reward them—reward them for results. . . . Life is about performing, being judged on that performance, and being rewarded or not rewarded based on your achievements. So when people achieve something, we reward them for it, have them feel good about it. And when they fail to achieve, privately discuss with them how it can be done better.

In addition to specific performance rewards, the Copperweld culture is also distinguished by a core value of recognition and celebration. While many corporations are cutting company picnics and other employee activities to save money, Copperweld actively looks for opportunities to celebrate. Its various plants continue to have social activities with families, and each location is given great autonomy in how it goes about doing so. In Fayetteville, Tennessee, employees hold barbecues and picnics. In Chicago they attend theme parks as a group. The company celebrated the twentieth anniversary of its "new" wire division. Weekly division publications recognize retirees and birthdays, offer condolences for deaths in employees' families, and celebrate marriages and births. Several survivors I interviewed used the term "the Copperweld family," a rare characterization in today's rapidly changing business environments.

### Provide Training and Other Resources

Copperweld's plants are state-of-the-art. This was a major postdownsizing, restructuring goal. The company made substantial investments in capital equipment and expansion, giving employees the best leading-edge technology, systems, and tools to work with. This has been coupled with an impressive commitment to training. In 1993, when the Shelby plant in Ohio rebuilt its seamless mill and installed new state-of-the-art German equipment, for example, Copperweld sent the employees who would maintain and operate the mill to Germany for intensive training. Similarly, as they installed a new Italian tube mill in the Miami Division, they backed up their investment by sending employees to the source, in Italy, for training.

Eugene Pocci, the vice president of human resources, speaks with great pride of his company's commitment to providing the training and technology needed to ensure a continuous movement toward excellence. He tells how, following the downsizing, he purchased a block of training hours that employees could sign up for at their discretion whenever they needed training. And employees we spoke with concurred: "There is no training that we need, that we can't access. All we have to do is say it would help us work better."

There is always a real and a perceived loss of competence following any restructuring, when people take on new jobs and an additional workload. Copperweld uses training as a way to restore the confidence and competence of its workforce as it repositions itself more competitively.

In Turner's words, "You give me five guys that are out there digging a hole with a hand shovel. They are working, they are sweating, they are giving you 110 percent. But that hole ain't getting very big fast. Take a backhoe out there with one *skilled* operator and you've got a hole in a heartbeat. That's why we give people the tools, and then train them to use them."

## SUMMARY OF LESSONS FROM COPPERWELD

- Stick to what you do best. Let the customer guide you.
- Cut quickly and deeply. Do it once.
- Be honest about the prognosis and compassionate about survivor anxiety.

- Let survivors know that they are valued and valuable to the company.
- Keep people informed, and be consistent in your message.
- To win trust, treat people fairly. But never take trust for granted.
- Put a positive spin on everything.
- Reward and celebrate people.
- Provide training and other resources as a means of empowerment.

# Chapter 5

—∿∿—

# THE PITTSBURGH POST-GAZETTE CASE

At the *Pittsburgh Post-Gazette* headquarters, we were greeted by a succession of busy, friendly employees who ushered us into managing editor Madelyn Ross's cluttered, cozy office. Ross, a local newspaper industry legend in her own right, had led "the reinvention of the *Pittsburgh Press*" with an emphasis on solid investigative reporting and strong writing. Now she faced the same challenge at the new *Post-Gazette* as a major player on a dedicated, visionary team of senior editors headed by John Craig.

Ross, like everyone we interviewed, was delighted to talk about the *Press/Post-Gazette* story. In the past she had allowed student groups, including my own graduate students at Carnegie Mellon University, to study the company and its latest transformation. It was clear that the newspaper business was her passion. We later learned from everyone we talked to that this passion informed her leadership style; she was dedicated, task oriented, focused, detail oriented, effective, and, as one editor later described her, "not given to loosey-goosey fraternizing, but open to input from others." This style, we also learned, appropriately complemented that of editor John Craig. In the eyes of his employees, Craig was less hands-on, more intuitive, less predictable, and more likely to express his expectations and then back off and "let things happen." Craig, they told us, had a penchant for stirring up a healthy conflict of ideas to spark creativity.

Ross greeted us warmly, was attentive to our needs, and at the same time seemed driven and results oriented. Without fanfare or small talk, she immediately whisked us off to the unpretentious newspaper-strewn conference room furnished with a huge battered wooden table and with chairs covered in shades of dirty. This is where we were to meet our first interviewees. Within minutes the first employees filed into the room. They were a high-energy, intense, very communicative group of *Post-Gazette* editors who openly shared their responses to our questions, often talking simultaneously. "So you want to hear about how the little fish swallowed up the big fish?" one of them queried as he took his seat.

This intriguing story of labor struggles, a merger, and an organizational rebirth had begun in 1961 when the two newspapers were wedded under an unusual agreement. The *Pittsburgh Press*, the larger of the two papers, was owned by the Pittsburgh Press Company, which in turn was owned by the E. W. Scripps Company of Cincinnati (later to evolve into the Scripps-Howard Company). The *Pittsburgh Post-Gazette*, the smaller, less popular of the two papers, was owned by Blade Communications, a Toledo-based Block family business. They came together under an agency agreement sanctioned by the Newspaper Preservation Act of 1963. Housed in the same building, the papers shared the Scripps-owned business operations, including production, marketing, advertisement, and distribution. The *Press* was thus the "business leader," taking primary responsibility for the administrative aspects of printing, publishing, distribution, advertising, and sales. The *Post-Gazette* was strictly a newsroom, focused mainly on the creative aspects of newspaper writing. But theirs was an uneasy alliance, marked by labor-management tensions, bitter rivalries for status and readership, and the ever present expectation that when the agreement expired on December 31, 1999, it would not be renewed.

It was generally assumed that in the year 2000 one of three

possible scenarios would occur: the *Post-Gazette* would simply close its doors forever, the *Press* would buy the *Post-Gazette* and they would merge as one company, or the *Post-Gazette* would be sold to an independent buyer. But none of that was to be. Through a series of unexpected turns of events, the unthinkable happened in 1993. The smaller, weaker company, the *Post-Gazette*, bought the *Press*.

This unexpected turn of events was precipitated by a bitter eight-month strike that made journalism history. In the early nineties the Scripps-Howard Company, faced with escalating labor costs, aging equipment, sluggish sales, and internal inefficiencies, began to reassess its Pittsburgh newspaper. Then, in December 1991, ten union contracts expired. Scripps-Howard, seizing the moment, unveiled an unpopular plan that called for dramatic changes in the papers' distribution system. Through consolidation of drop-off points, the plan would eliminate 450 Teamsters and displace 4,300 boys and girls who delivered papers. The plan did not sit well in a city steeped in tradition about such matters, and the May 17, 1992, strike that felled both newspapers was, some say, inevitable.

Newly formed and fledgling suburban newspapers rushed in to fill the void. Television journalists intensified their reporting. All of this compounded the situation for Scripps-Howard. The company played hardball for a while, advertising in other cities for temporary replacement workers, which only further outraged the union-loyal Pittsburgh community. It didn't help when the papers, "after having fired the children," threatened to resume publication with or without the striking workers. On that day, July 27, the city of Pittsburgh canceled all police leaves in anticipation of the fallout from the decision.

After the bitter standoff, tentative negotiations, and sporadic incidences of violence, the worn-out Scripps' negotiators finally threw in the towel and sought a buyer for the papers. In October it was announced that the Block family, already the owner of the *Post-Gazette*, would buy the *Post*. At the end of December, after all the deals had been worked out, including stipulations for the phasing out of 260 Teamster jobs over five years and the necessary approvals from the U.S. Department of Justice, John Craig began the challenging job of assembling a new, integrated management team and staff to begin the process of healing and transforming the new *Post-Gazette*.

As one would expect, the familiar scenes of survivor anguish that are the subject of this book repeated themselves at the new *Post-Gazette*. But with these came unique strategies that warrant the company's inclusion as a success story. First, there was the Staff Merger Committee and, then, the decision to adopt comanagers—one from the old *Press* paired with one from the old *Post-Gazette*. There was also the decision on the part of Craig and his staff to create a new culture that embodied the best of both former papers' cultures.

## MANAGING THE AFTERSHOCKS

### *The Editors' Story*

The *Post-Gazette* editors spoke in rapid-fire sequences, their ideas often merging into consensus as they reminisced about the events of the previous two or three years. At times they recalled with amusement the critical events that had reshaped their company and their careers. At other times they recalled the agony of waiting for the next unforeseeable turn of events. The editors recollected the immediate aftermath of the acquisition as though it had been moments ago:

> [When] Scripps-Howard announced that they were going to sell the newspaper, I think the general perception was "Oh, God, just don't let it be to the *Post-Gazette*!" because we thought the rivalry between us would result in a massacre of *Press* people if the *Post-Gazette* bought the paper. And then about three weeks later the *Post-Gazette* did buy the *Press*. That caused great anguish and tears in the newsroom and things like that. It was a strange situation having a For Sale sign around your neck. And there were rumors. Someone said they saw

Tony Ridder of Knight down on the Boulevard of the Allies or something. At one point somebody's spouse who worked at the *Wall Street Journal* called into the newsroom and said that Tony Ridder made it official that he wasn't interested in the *Press*. So there was this wide-swept panic around.

I remember Maddy Ross, the managing editor, going from department to department saying officially, "Don't worry." At that point we were about to collapse with worry. So there was a lot of fear and trepidation when the *Post-Gazette* bought the paper.

We were competitors. I too was with the *Press* and suffered anguish and anxiety about what would happen next. The *Press* had instituted a program called "Save the *Press*." We held a few news conferences. We wore ["Save the *Press*"] T-shirts and such. And I can remember thinking as a member of the *Press* that this was a nice gesture. It wouldn't go anyplace, but it represented the feelings of the staff. I happened to go upstairs, and I saw our logo, "Save the *Press*," turned into "Buy the *Press*" on a *Post-Gazette* wall. It was clearly because they suffered from the same anguish, the same anxieties. But they had a totally different take on it. If the *Press* were to be sold to Knight-Ridder, they would be out of jobs. So it was a trying situation for both sides.

I think what we *Post-Gazette* people were hoping for during the strike was to continue the status quo. Unlike the *Press*, most of our people had been laid off. We had a handful of management types that were working on busywork more or less. We were basically just hoping to keep the status quo.

One editor described the inevitable cultural clash this way:

The cultures of the two papers were very different. The *Post-Gazette* was smaller, and in its general tone more egalitarian. It was a less hierarchical structure in terms of the relationship of managers to reporters. It was looser both in the good sense and in a bad sense—it was able to move more quickly and to be more creative, but it also suffered from being poorly organized or unfocused at times. The *Press* was more businesslike, more organized. We at the *Post-Gazette* didn't worry much about production and business matters; we only had to worry about our editorial operation. And we all knew the *Press* took some pride in propping us up financially. The Sunday paper, for example, was the big revenue generator that kept all of us alive. The culture of the *Press* came from its role—being the one that bore the responsibility, being in charge, being the dominant paper. We thought of ourselves as the feisty, quality underdog. Our culture at the *Post-Gazette* was also shaped by our awareness that at any moment things might fall apart for us and we might all have to go elsewhere.

## The Reporters' Story

"We are in charge of ourselves. We are reporters," offered a member of this group when, on entering the room, I asked to be reminded which group I was about to interview. I explained my purpose and distributed a written survey designed to measure survivor attitudes. The reporters talked casually and openly, comparing notes as they filled out the questionnaire:

"There was one year where a lot of us weren't working at all. We were laid off because of the strike. I guess the *Press* people were still working, though."

"We lost our jobs and thought we were goners. We didn't have any paychecks, but the *Press* people were paid for eight months."

"In the course of the strike, people went from extremely high levels of confidence and job satisfaction down to nil."

[Sarcastically] "In one of the cleverest moves in the business, the *Pittsburgh Press* went out of business and somehow still seems to have acquired the *Post-Gazette!*"

These were men and women of many words. They talked in stream of consciousness. They talked in unison, finishing one another's thoughts as they weaved together an intricate story of twists and unpredictable turns.

In essence what happened was, when the *Press* was slowly sinking staff writers, reporters at the *Press* were feeling fairly confident that a great many of them were going to be taken on because the *P-G* was going to need reporters and the *P-G* had pretty much signaled commitment to hire specifically from the pool of *Press* reporters. Which knowing the *Press's* management, I am certain the *Pittsburgh Press* would not have done that if the situation had been turned around the other way. And the first shock was that the *Post-Gazette* seemed to have hired an extraordinary number of editors from the *Press*. I mean in surprising numbers from the copy desk all the way through the ranks. And I know that that was one of the first things that created a certain amount of tension as the merger got under way.

The other part of it was that at the same time we were melding the two staffs among the reporters there were competitive wounds showing. In which case we had *Pittsburgh Press* reporters lamenting the demise of their own paper and the uncertainty of their own futures, and they felt there were a number of very good staffers here for whom no room was found.

On the other hand there were a number of good *Post-Gazette* reporters who were looking and commenting rather openly about the extent to which *Press* managers were hired for the news operation and who bore a considerable amount of resentment because they had spent almost a full year without a complete paycheck and almost no economic certainty as a result of management decisions made by people like Jimmy Manis and Bill Burleigh and a number of other people in Cincinnati who are going to go to hell when they die. That was pretty much what the two staffs as I see it were presented with as they prepared to merge.

Thus, the merging of these two cultures, apart from the predictable pain of any such restructuring, created enormous anxieties that had their roots in a clash of values, styles, and expectations. To compound matters, there were new resentments on both sides. The *Post-Gazette* reporters had been laid off during the strike. They came back to work feeling bitter about having had to live on tight budgets while the *Press* employees were kept on the payroll. Later, however, about half of the *Press* employees were cut, so that the *Press* survivors came into the new *Post-Gazette* organization feeling insecure, anxious, and distrustful of the new order.

## The Senior Staff's Story

Madelyn Ross, Matt Kennedy, and Mike McGough were, like the reporters, open, thoughtful, and eager:

> . . . I think the strike was such an emotionally wrenching thing for both groups of people that, when we came together and needed to put out a newspaper within three weeks, all of these emotional issues, and try to heal, we had no time really to give it any exclusive attention because pressing down on us was this deadline. And what we needed to do just to get a paper out . . . that part was nearly overwhelming. We had the staff on two different floors of the building, and we had to physically relocate the *Post-Gazette* to this floor. All the computers, all of the furniture, all of their personal effects had to be moved and relocated, and we wanted to rearrange all of the *Press* people's desks and furniture so they wouldn't be sitting in the same seat that they sat in when the *Press* died. So it was a symbolic transition. New. Everything here was to be new. We didn't even know at that point what sections of the paper we would have or if we would have a features section or a business section. We didn't know. It was reinventing a newspaper from scratch.

> You have to understand that by and large most of the major metropolitan daily newspapers in this country have been on a plane of momentum for generations. So 80 percent of what happens each day is a function of deeply ingrained, almost nervous system kinds of response because problems have been identified, nailed down, and solved in some cases years ago. Rightly or not, for good or ill, this is how it is. So suddenly we had this really interesting situation where nothing is nailed down. The managing editor said we didn't even know what sections would be titles or what the content was going to be in

those sections. I mean that is an unthinkable situation to be in as a journalist for a large metro paper because . . .

Three weeks before you are supposed to be on the street.

I mean it was just unthinkable. If someone had sat down and made a list of all the things that would have to be thought through and all the tasks that had to be accomplished before the newspaper returned, I think a considered outsider looking at that would say it wasn't possible.

It was impossible. We didn't know who was covering what. We had, because of the way the staff was formed, we had beats with two reporters on them and other beats with no reporters on them. So we had to completely reevaluate the staffing, who was going to go where and how to approach that emotional situation, because a lot of these beat reporters had been in those beats for years at one or the other paper and now we are saying, "We really like you and want you to be on the staff, but you cannot be on the beat because somebody else already has it."

I can't think of anything that wasn't thrown up into the air.

One of my last jobs at the old *Press* was working on the outplacement efforts. And when I was hired to start working at the new *P-G*, it was a mad scramble to locate enough text-editing terminals to have the equipment physically located, wired, and checked and ready to go to even type things.

Symbolic of what seemed to be chaos was [the fact that] the day before the staff was supposed to sit down in the newsroom and begin creating a newspaper the newsroom was totally torn apart. The desks weren't in place [and] there were wires hanging from the ceiling. It looked like a bomb had gone off. There weren't enough phones. The phones weren't connected. And this was the day before. And somehow that day and through that night we put it together [with] some of the staff, which, by the way, was incredibly helpful and resilient through all of this. Some of the staff members had even gone so far as to buy little plants for each desk as a welcoming thing. Somehow by the next morning when they walked into work they arrived to a newsroom that was pristine and even had little plants on the desks. It truly was a miracle.

The spectacle of chaos, and the metaphor of bombs exploding while the walking wounded sought ways to heal themselves sufficiently to achieve an impossible mission, was in sharp contrast to this last comment about "little plants on the desks" and miraculous outcomes.

The senior staff offered two possible reasons for their success. One was the fact that, faced with the immediacy of the task to produce a paper, people rose to the occasion, "much like people who have experienced death," suggested one of the senior editors. "The routine might have been a blessing. People had to heal themselves to get moving." The other critical variable was the presence of the employee-led Staff Merger Committee anointed by the new management team. Their first charge was to join management in its efforts to promote healing of the merged, downsized, reinvented *Post-Gazette* organization.

## HEALING THE WOUNDS

Research tells us that people in any transition are likely to resist the new order for a variety of reasons. For one thing there is a loss of control as familiar structures and patterns of interacting and performing give way to new ones. The new *Post-Gazette* had only seventeen days to restructure its entire office and to forge new relationships that involved the melding of two cultures into one. Management was faced with the enormous task of reinstating all of the old *Post-Gazette* employees and eighty-three *Press* employees, moving all equipment and furniture into the reconfigured office space, reassigning reporters and managers in ways that avoided duplication of efforts, and getting the job done effectively.

In addition to this restructuring challenge, management was faced with dealing with the reality that all transitions pose a crisis of identity for those affected. In this case both former *Press* employees and returning *Post-Gazette* employees had to bear the painful process of redefining their roles and rebuilding their self-esteem in the new organization.

Healing these wounds was no easy task, especially in a climate in which the community was angry at the newspaper and the staffs on both sides, who had become bitter rivals, had to move past their fears and resentments to become a high performing team. Many *Press* staffers felt like prisoners of war in the *Post-Gazette* territory. Trust was a major casualty in both camps, and the stereotypical cynicism of journalists had been well fueled by the treatment from Scripps-Howard during the strike. Management's major challenge was deciding what salve to apply to repair the damage done to people's psyche so that they could recuperate sufficiently to rebuild the newspaper.

In addition, the newspaper was being assaulted by the external environment. Fifteen competitors had sprung up during the strike to attempt to grab market share. They included both print and electronic media vying for the former readership of both papers. In this all-out war the challenge was clear: coalesce quickly or die.

## LESSONS FROM THE PITTSBURGH POST-GAZETTE

In managing these losses and wounds, the *Post-Gazette* transitional management team made the following smart moves that can be lessons for all of us.

### *Acknowledge Employees' Losses and Allow Grieving*

Several years ago Elisabeth Kübler-Ross made a major contribution to our understanding of the grieving and healing process associated with death and dying. Since then, her five-stage process has been applied to understanding the journey we must take in resolving any loss, including not only the tragedy of losing a loved one but also that of losing our jobs, our security, or even the familiar embedded in positive life events like marriages or promotions. The research and literature dealing with downsizing survivors consistently makes reference to Kübler-Ross's work. We are reminded that being laid off or surviving a layoff is a major life event and, like all critical life events, holds losses for those involved. Such losses must be acknowledged and grieving must occur before healing can take place.

According to the Kübler-Ross model, our journey toward wholeness following a loss moves from shock and denial to anger, then bargaining, then depression, and finally acceptance. Of course, people can and do get stuck at any one of these stages. Some people, for example, get mired in chronic denial. Unable to admit that they have experienced a loss, they are never able to come to terms with the necessary healing and release of pent-up anxiety. Others get hopelessly stuck in their anger. We see this daily as some survivors are never able to get past the outrage they feel at the organization. As a result they eventually become too demoralized and demotivated to function effectively at work.

*Post-Gazette* senior managers scored many points with those we interviewed for their attempts to promote survivor healing by giving employees "permission" to express anguish about their loss of identity and security and to voice their concerns about their future. They did not fall into the trap that so many managers do of saying prematurely, "Things are going to be fine. Let's get back to work." Instead, the *Post-Gazette* senior management team actively sought advice from external consultants and their own employees on ways to enable a grieving and healing process. They understood that denial is a natural first response that serves the purpose of buffering the full force of the shock of loss. They also understand the importance of moving people away from denial to the next stages on the grieving continuum. Anger, stage two, was encouraged rather than suppressed. As one reporter put it,

> We were allowed to vent our anger. We had a committee. I forget what it was called. . . . We met in the conference room down in the mezzanine. The meeting at one point was so acrimonious that everybody wanted to join the committee to come

and see the fights. But it was to smooth away and try to talk over some of the problems we foresaw. . . . The first thing was that people vented their hostilities. There was some union posturing about "Where am I going to land, and what is going to happen to my job?" But then we moved forward and said, "How are we going to become one staff?"

Employees and managers understood intuitively that the way to get past anger was to express it. They were then freed up to move to the third stage of grieving: bargaining. This is reflected in the last line of the reporter's comments above: "But then we moved forward and said, 'How are we going to become one staff?' " The bargaining process at the *Post-Gazette* was an intriguing one. Certain questions became the basis for negotiations and clarification about the future: What is my job now? How do I interact with the new managers? What are the differences between the way things worked in my former job and the way they work in the new organization? What will I have to do, or to do differently, in order to survive? These questions captured the anxiety experienced when employees who used to know what to expect and how things worked were suddenly challenged to renew themselves as their organization transformed itself into an as yet unknown entity. But the questions could be asked and answered effectively only after the shock, denial, and anger were expressed.

Management consistently demonstrated a willingness to work with employees to find win-win solutions to these questions. In so doing, employees were able to move to the next stage: depression, marked by low morale and feelings of isolation and of being overwhelmed. In entering this stage people dealing with loss often become hopeless. They think, I've dealt with my anger and my loss; why do I feel bad? What they often fail to realize is that the depression signals a "settling in," a necessary step on the way to the final stage: acceptance. A group of editors reflecting on this period talked about the sobering impact of the realization that "we had better keep our resumes ready" because "there's no such thing as security."

## Create a Healing Environment

The most important intervention in the grieving process described above was the creation of the Staff Merger Committee, an employee-led group set up by senior management to give employees a forum to mourn their losses and begin to heal themselves. As a senior editor put it, "We felt it was important for the staff to take charge of their own healing and find out what they needed to do to recover." Once the committee was installed, senior management stepped back and allowed the members to develop their own ideas and run with them.

The Staff Merger Committee met for an hour at a time, on company time. The early meetings became a forum for grieving, which took the form of expressions of anger over the situation of the previous year. *Post-Gazette* employees and former *Press* employees fought loudly over who had been hurt worse by the strike. But in time the group moved from griping to grappling with their differences. Thus began a healing process, which continues today, as employees began to focus on their purpose: "to create a unified staff and plan for the move into the 'new' newsroom" previously occupied by the *Press.*

The committee implemented several actions, some symbolic, some pragmatic. For example, it decided to put plants on all employees' desks in the newly arranged newsroom as a token of welcome and cheer. It also organized a luncheon for the newsroom staff. At the luncheon all editors stood up and introduced themselves one by one. The people from the Toledo headquarters came and introduced themselves. The luncheon and accompanying activities signified to the newsroom staff that they were part of a new family. Unified in the fellowship of shared meals, the two somewhat estranged groups took meaningful steps toward becoming one.

The members of the Staff Merger Committee we interviewed generally had a positive outlook concerning the new organization. Participating on the committee, they told us, allowed them to air their grievances and, perhaps more important, gave them something positive to do to create their new culture.

## Encourage Employees to Heal Themselves

"The key," said Madelyn Ross, "is getting everyone involved from the start. The only reason in my estimation that these very different groups, both heartbroken for one reason or another, could work together so quickly . . . is because they were involved in creating their new organization. We sort of handed it off to them, but they took it and ran. They took the initiative to get groups together to decide what plants to put on the desk." And the significance of this gesture was not missed by Ross. She added, "The plants were a sort of symbol here. Their discussions ranged much deeper and were far more wide-ranging than just arranging plants on desks."

Managers at the *Post-Gazette* are quick to point out that employees actively took charge of their own recovery. And this is significant. In the downsizing organizations we encounter, we have learned that healing cannot be "done to" employees by managers. At some point each employee must become a full participant in getting his or her own needs met. As Ross put it, "John Craig and I both had some ideas in the very early days, as did all the other managers, about how to get them to come together. We really simply set up the opportunities and then got out of the way. It was the staff who did it. Had they not done it, we would have been in a real mess."

When we met with the editors, we asked how they had managed to heal following the merger and its necessary losses. The first comment out of this group referred to the employee-led Staff Merger Committee: "I was part of a kiss-and-make-up group. We would come together for one hour at a time. It was a huge room; you couldn't remember the names. So we broke into different groups to bring us together. It really worked eventually."

The reporters told a similar story: "What we did was we had a big lunch for everybody and all the managers; the editor, Mr.

Block, me, and some other people that I didn't know, we all planned this lunch. We came in the first day and we had *P-G* coffee cups. They took the *Post-Gazette* yellow and *Press* blue and made our corporate color green."

"It was a pretty damn good thing. They called it 'the dawn of a new era.' It was an esprit de corps thing. It was nice to get that close to John Craig."

"They had several get-togethers even before that party, in a bar close to here. . . . It was really good for me because I was basically in a state of mourning, and really for about the first year I was here walking around like 'this is a nightmare, I want to wake up,' even though there were some things about my new job I actually liked better."

## Proactively Manage Cultural Change

Perhaps the most pressing challenge of any merger is the challenge of diagnosing, melding, and re-creating a corporate culture that supports people in achieving the new vision and goals. Staffers from both former organizations agreed on the contrasts between the *Press* and *Post-Gazette* cultures. The *Press*, they told us, was larger, more efficient, and more control oriented, and it embodied more of a traditional, top-down "classic" newsroom structure, in which decisions such as clearance to use the word "hell," for example, had to be secured from the managing editor. The old *Post-Gazette*, in contrast, was smaller, more intimate, more inefficient, less formal, less bureaucratic, and more spontaneous in its decision-making processes. The goal of senior management in leading the merger was to capitalize on the best both cultures had to offer. At the same time they had to resolve a pressing related dilemma: "how to be true to ourselves and to our commitment to the community?"

John Craig and Madelyn Ross spent countless hours during the transition discussing questions of ethics, values, and philosophy, both privately and in employee sessions, as they envisioned and shaped the new entity. They specifically reflected on the following questions: What is our journalism about? Who are we now? What are we about? What core values, beliefs, and principles on both sides will drive us into the future? Their search led to an emerging new culture carrying the best of the old and attempting to blend both around the task at hand. Craig and Ross retained the top management of both newspapers and made clever compromises, like appointing two top managers, one from the former *Press* and one from the old *Post-Gazette*, to head each new department. In effect, Craig and Ross created a new/old paper with a shared history. The emerging culture was reliable, trustworthy, and predictable, yet alert and flexible.

## *Involve Employees in Decisions Affecting Them*

According to Madelyn Ross, through frequent planning meetings management made every effort to include employees. Once staffers were hired, they were expected to participate in all aspects of the effort to change. While employees might not have been aware of this, they were more involved in the day-to-day implementation of the new organization than is typical in most organizations undergoing this sort of upheaval and a merger. Employee involvement was also made easier by the fact that those who returned to work at the new *Post-Gazette* were willing and eager to make things work. Once employees got past the competitive wound, they showed that the two staffs—from the former *Press* and old *Post-Gazette*—could put their heads together to figure out how to move forward. Everybody pitched in, even to do mundane tasks like moving desks. Several got together at local bars to socialize. Work plans were often the subject of these informal sessions.

Counseling was made available to staffers who were having difficulty sorting through things and who needed support in making the transition. This was part of an honest acknowledgment that there were still unresolved issues. For example, many reporters still feel that the dual-manager arrangement is dysfunctional. It's not always clear who calls the shots or whether all the power struggles of the past have been resolved. And there are still pockets of "venting clubs" as people continue to tend to their wounds.

What is clear, though, is the fact that people are generally working well together. In listing their successes, *Post-Gazette* reporters who are union members talked openly about managers being more supportive and inclusive of reporters. In their words, they feel more trusted and more empowered to act than before. They refer to the newspaper as "family oriented" and "considerate of personal needs," and they acknowledge that the new, flatter organization allows for more flexibility and creativity and for quicker reaction times.

## Allow the Work to Become a Rallying Point

Organizations that heal themselves following downsizing and restructuring consistently balance the need to tend to the wounds with an intensive focus on the tasks at hand. As I interviewed companies for inclusion in this book, employees at all levels repeatedly commented on the healing role that work itself can play as people struggle to regain equilibrium following an upheaval in their work lives.

The need to put out a paper in a few days became a battle cry for the leadership of the new *Post-Gazette*, and it was the force that energized employees to heal their differences by coalescing into a high performing team. While some organizations stage "Outward Bound" experiences in the wilderness to give employees the opportunity to explore teamwork and build team skills, the *Post-Gazette* was serendipitously thrown into a series of crises that became rallying points for healing.

There was the event during the first week of the new *Post-Gazette's* operation that is referred to internally by some as the "Bill Clinton odyssey." Dennis Roddy, a former *Press* reporter, and Diana Nelson Jones, a *Post-Gazette* reporter, were thrown together on a trip on which they trailed President Clinton wherever he went during his inauguration. They cowrote what turned out to be an excellent story, and the double byline of these two reporters became an early symbol of the unification of the two cultures.

Then, in September 1994, there occurred the tragic crash of USAir Flight 427, which unified the city of Pittsburgh as a family in mourning and had a similar effect on the recuperating *Post-Gazette* family. Here is one editor's account:

> I have never seen an organization perform like this one. The crash happened Thursday night. The next day we had to decide what to do from here, plus plan the Sunday paper. John [Craig] called everyone in and said he wanted an entire special section devoted to the crash. Friday at 1 A.M. we had located seven victims' families. By Saturday afternoon we had every victim's name and personal stories on twenty-nine victims. Department barriers fell apart. Everyone came out with greater feelings of teamwork than ever before.

Both events are examples of the power of crisis and the challenge of the work ahead as restorative forces when an organization reinvents itself. As Matt Kennedy, assistant to the editor, put it, ". . . we needed to focus very quickly on concrete, professional, work-oriented things. Focusing our energy on things that were achievable, doable — things you could look at the next day and realize 'well that got done,' as opposed to have a lot of energy floating around just attaching itself to whatever." Kennedy later added, "Some organizations spend a heck of a lot of money to throw people on rubber rafts to go down the Colorado, having them climb mountains and things . . ." to which Madelyn Ross responded, "We live the raft."

These stories and observations reinforce what true survivors at the *Post-Gazette* consistently suggested — the work and the importance of the journalism became the overarching factor in promoting their healing.

# SUMMARY OF LESSONS FROM THE PITTSBURGH POST-GAZETTE

- Acknowledge employees' losses and allow grieving.
- Create a healing environment.
- Encourage employees to take responsibility for their own recovery.
- Proactively manage cultural change.
- Involve employees in decisions affecting them.
- Allow the work to become a rallying point.

## SURVIVOR CLOSE-UP

Edwina Kaikai epitomizes the new workforce: metropolitan editor of Pittsburgh's largest newspaper, mother of a preschooler, Cicely, a first grader, Edward, and a step-son, Christian, who is a high school junior. She is a wife, dutiful daughter, and a person who is community minded and socially active. She is complex and refreshing, with a blend of amiable people skills and the toughness of a hard-nosed reporter, caring supervisor and no-nonsense business decision maker, professional mentor and second-shift homemaker. Like working parents everywhere who survive downsizing, she navigates the rapidly evolving business world seeking equilibrium in her career and family life. Many survivors seek this balance by separating work and family life into opposing camps. Kaikai's approach is a masterful example of a blended existence. Her life is woven together by a series of choices designed to maintain her equilibrium.

I interviewed Kaikai on January 18, 1996, the third anniversary of the new *Post-Gazette*, in the small cagelike office from which she surveys the newsroom through the slatted blinds of a small window. In the corner between the wall and her huge computer, New Age self-help books for black women share a cramped space with professional manuals. "How to have both a job and a life I love" is how she describes the values that drive her in the aftermath of her company's rebirth. Not one to go past where she's happiest, Kaikai notes, "I want opportunities to grow here. I look at my colleagues elsewhere who have gone for stardom professionally but have no life, and I cringe. I have turned down attractive job opportunities, including one as feature editor of a large newspaper. It was enticing, but it would upset my family balance."

She came to the *Pittsburgh Press* straight out of Temple University's journalism program, vowing to "Be twice as good, work twice as hard, be as close to perfect as I could be, in order to be taken seriously," in spite of her minority status as a twenty-one-year-old African American woman. "On assignments I asked every question that could possibly come to mind, because there was to be no doubt that I was good. Facts right, story right every time—willingly going the extra mile, working every shift. I would never, ever consider cutting corners like some reporters do. I was consumed with being excellent, moved by my personal drive to be the best I could be."

Kaikai moved smoothly from assignment to assignment—promotions, compensation, recognition. She became a utility player—someone management felt comfortable sending to do many different kinds of assignments. In 1982 Madelyn Ross suggested that she fill in on the city desk temporarily as assistant city editor. This was a career highlight. Being an editor is the prize for newspaper journalists. It is not often offered to someone in the first decade of a career. She was flying high, doing work she loved, getting outstanding performance reviews, getting more and more responsibility. Nothing prepared her for what happened next. The job of assistant city editor was formally created. It was given to someone else.

Through her tears she spoke of the event fourteen years earlier that had foreshadowed her second career crisis—the sale of the *Press* to the *Post-Gazette:* "I was crushed. I was pissed. I was outraged—betrayed. My father, who was dying of cancer, was calm and comforting. He taught me the most important lesson of my career. He said, 'All things in time. Go over and congratulate the person who was given the job and carry on.' It was tough, but that's exactly what I did after asking the managing editor to explain his decision."

In 1983 Kaikai was named the *Press*'s East editor. She assumed the position a wiser, less starry-eyed professional. Following what was for her the most blatant encounter with job discrimination she had ever experienced, she vowed never to expect a fair shake in business. But she maintained her motivation by keeping her father's words in mind: "All things in time."

In 1987 she got married. Four years later she was a mother of two children, juggling many balls, and loving the experience:

> I had a great marriage, two kids, an excellent job doing exactly what I wanted to be doing with the biggest newspaper in my hometown city. I lived four doors down from my mom, who baby-sits my children while I work. My husband was comfortable in his job. I passed up many offers from colleagues in other cities for exciting positions that would bring more money and better opportunities. But I wanted to remain in Pittsburgh, enjoying the wonderful security I had created in my work and family life.

Then the strike of May 1992 hit. Its seriousness was met with denial. Like everyone else, Kaikai thought in time that the differences would be resolved. When the strike dragged on, her anxiety grew as she recalled the shock of losing the assistant city editor job ten years earlier and reflected on her financial responsibilities as a parent. Panic set in when the *Post-Gazette* purchased the *Press* and she, like others, had to interview with the new *Post-Gazette*.

Kaikai recalled her father's comforting words, now echoed uncannily by her husband's: "Don't worry about what you cannot change. Just make sure you're prepared to take advantage of other opportunities." I pointed out the similarity between the two significant men in her life. She agreed. "Unfortunately they never got to meet each other. They were both calm, trusting in the universe." We reflected on the importance of this worldview for survivors of today's constantly changing work environments. We reflected on the importance of having stabilizing support networks like her family, past mentors, and current boss, who is encouraging and supportive of her choices. Then she added,

> I have managed to survive in a job I love. My personal and professional life work together well, but it's not always a perfect balance. As I head for the kitchen to start dinner, I often wish there were more hours in the day. I'd love to have my kids in bed by 8 P.M. Instead at 8 we're eating dinner. On a good night they retire at 10. Now I'm working on having personal time for myself. So I get up at 5:30 A.M. to exercise. I go to bed at 11:30 P.M., but my husband is a night person so I steal time from him. My mother was right: women who are teachers have it better. But that's not my choice. The newspaper business is my choice.

## Chapter 6

—✺—

# THE ONONDAGA
# COMMUNITY COLLEGE CASE

When Bruce Leslie assumed the leadership of Onondaga Community College (OCC) in 1984, he was greeted by the managerial dilemma of the decade. Government funding cuts, a declining enrollment, the growth of the technology, and the escalating expenses of campus management all pointed in one direction: increase the enrollment and cut costs.

OCC is not unique in this respect. Institutions of higher learning everywhere are being assaulted by the same forces that have invaded government, business, and industry. They must find creative new ways to secure operating dollars and cut costs. They must provide the right mix of competitive skills for the workforce of the future, reshaping the traditional menu of humanities and science degrees. They must see to the reeducation of faculty. They must compete with remote computer-aided and satellite-beamed educational options and with accredited business-minded proprietary schools that offer financial aid, relevant technical certificates, and job placement after ten months instead of two or four years.

In response to these new challenges, colleges are scrambling to change themselves. Many now outsource services such as custodial maintenance and benefits administration in an effort to cut costs and become viable profit centers. Some are making even bolder moves. According to a 1995 *New York*

*Times* "Magazine" article, Elizabeth Coleman, the president of Bennington College in Vermont, now challenges her faculty to be what they do. She has determined that, to be competitive, faculty members must work at their crafts, not just teach about them. She makes such proclamations as she strips away the traditional sacred notion of tenure, sending the clear message that there is no more business as usual. In this brave new world of academia, faculty and staff who are out of sync with the demands of the workplace may face obsolescence. The demise of the organization man, a legacy of the reinvention of business, may well find a counterpart in higher education: the collapse of the security once enjoyed by tenured academics and administrative lifers.

Experience had taught Leslie that leading the necessary transition would be no easy task. As a rule academic institutions are slow to change the way they do business. Like many colleges in the area, OCC had a history rooted in tenure rights, job security, and union contracts that made layoffs and restructuring virtually impossible. But Leslie forged doggedly ahead, paving the way for change and in the process providing us with a story of the pain of transition and of trial-and-error remedies for healing wounds and rebuilding morale. The lessons learned at OCC comprise an emerging picture of how to live and work through the chaos of change in a culture that has been fiercely committed to upholding traditions which may become obsolete in the near future. This is also a story of the personal journey of an academic leader faced with a wave of internal pressures and political constraints and how he sought to involve the staff and faculty in healing their losses by embracing "new beginnings."

Sitting on 180 acres of serene, bucolic land on the outskirts of Syracuse, OCC strikes the first-time visitor as a serene oasis unruffled by the stormy economic climate of New York State. On the surface there are no symptoms that the shock waves of downsizing and restructuring felt in government and industry also reverberate through the hallways of this successful community college.

The college was founded in 1961 as one of thirty two-year colleges in the State University of New York system. It has come a long way since its humble beginnings with five hundred students at Midtown Plaza in downtown Syracuse. Today it boasts an enrollment of over eight thousand students. Under the able leadership of Leslie, OCC is an institution poised for a dramatic competitive leap into the twenty-first century, fueled by its attention to the demands of high technology and the needs of a global economy. The vision statement says it well: "Onondaga Community College will be a visible resource, partner and leader in transforming education, students and the community for success in our rapidly changing world." The college affirms a commitment to small classes, individualized attention to its students, and pluralism that reflects society's cultural richness. Among its stated core values is a devotion to quality, caring, respect, and trust "as the foundation for lifelong individual growth and community development." On my first visit to the campus, faculty and senior administrators spoke with reverence and anticipation of the plans for a new state-of-the-art Applied Technology Center. A collaborative undertaking between the college and the business community, the technology center has become a symbol of Leslie's forward thinking stance.

In stark contrast to their seemingly stable, unperturbed environment, the faculty and staff members I met with told personal stories of their survivor anguish and their concerns for their future. They spoke of losses and uncertainty and of their fears of losing ground to high technology. They spoke with trepidation of eroding funding sources at the state and county levels, and, like survivors in organizations everywhere, some lamented the loss of certainty of the "good old days."

When I met with Leslie over breakfast at the Syracuse Inn, I was immediately reminded of management theorist Peter Drucker, who has drawn many useful parallels between the managerial challenges in industry and those in the not-for-profit sector. Drucker is quoted in a February 1993 issue of the *Wall Street Journal* as reminding us that "whenever a business keeps going downhill despite . . . heroic efforts by its people, the most likely cause is the obsolescence of its business theory." Leslie spoke a lot about the obsolescence of old ways of running colleges. He spoke with great sincerity and passion about building a true learning organization in which faculty members "model the way" as they lead change in the way work gets done. In his words, "Our challenge is the same as all organizations today. We must completely rethink the way we do business if we are to survive."

Leslie is a man of vision. His colleagues describe him as loyal, hardworking, decisive—sometimes to the point of being command oriented—and extremely committed to the cause of higher education. Yet, his penchant for getting the job done is balanced by a devotion to developing and applying effective interpersonal and leadership skills. He is sincere about listening to the concerns of his faculty and staff, taking great pains to return phone calls and maintain an open-door policy. Even the most disgruntled faculty members I spoke with were quick to add comments like "Bruce has feelings; he cares."

When he went to Onondaga from Prairie State College in Chicago Heights, Illinois, Leslie quickly established himself in the Syracuse community, where he founded the Year Round Syracuse Youth Corps and serves on numerous corporate and civic boards. He is well known for his professional expertise in leadership, workforce, and economic development, and he has earned such honors as Paul Laurence Dunbar Golden Poet Award and the Urban League's Harriet Tubman Corporate Award. In higher education circles Leslie has also won many accolades, including the Community College Trustees Association's Chief Executive Award.

In considering today's educational issues, Leslie is guided by an awareness of the challenges and opportunities posed by global competition and technology and by the pressing need to train the existing and future workforce to global standards. In our interview he repeatedly spoke of developing "good teachers," "good health care workers," "good employees," and "good students." Asked to define "good," he quickly answered, "people who have a willingness to embrace lifelong learning and retooling." It is in this spirit that he grants and encourages sabbaticals to develop existing faculty members in new content areas and makes innovative attempts to build education and training into day-to-day professional activities at the college. He views academic institutions as true learning organizations only if faculty members are able to work together effectively in teams, creating an environment that is an exemplary model for students to emulate as they develop their own work ethic.

But this is not the kind of work environment that Leslie found when he went to OCC. In addition to the dilemma of needing to do more with less, he inherited inefficient layers of administration. And as a longtime faculty member described it, "Bruce inherited a politically charged environment that had a history of bitterness, fear of reprisals, and strong factions."

Staffing represents 80 to 85 percent of the budget of the typical college. At the start of Leslie's tenure, there were 225 full-time faculty members and 341 adjunct faculty members at OCC for an enrollment of approximately 5,475 students. In addition, OCC employed 39 administrators and 194 civil service employees. Rather than anticipating continued enrollment growth, demographers at the time were predicting a lull in enrollment because of the ending of the baby boom. In fact, as a signal of the trend, school districts in the area were closing some elementary schools.

Clearly, in light of this, the 15–1 student-faculty ratio at OCC was indefensible. In fact, in areas such as laboratory courses and classes in music and the health professions the ratio was much smaller. In music, for example, ensembles of two or three students might provide a substantial part of a faculty member's load. In the health professions accrediting bodies and hospitals required certain student-faculty ratios, especially where safety was an issue. Some of these stipulations had been negotiated and were binding with the faculty union, providing very little flexibility for the college even if creative ways of addressing accreditation requirements could be found.

The union contract, however, did allow the administration

to establish class sizes in consultation with faculty chairs. But faculty chairs considered themselves coordinators, not administrators of their departments. While they maintained authority, they tended to disassociate themselves from the responsibilities an administrator would normally assume. All departments reported to the academic vice president, a span of control too great to effect much influence or oversight. Each department functioned autonomously, and the vice president accepted their decisions regarding staffing and curriculum. These decisions often influenced the staffing needs and levels in each department.

In addition to these structural and political constraints, the college had a large tenured faculty, most of whom had been hired in the sixties, when the college was founded. Most were in their mid-40s, so there was little or no prospect for a reduction in workforce by attrition. Tenured faculty members tend to spend their entire remaining career in the college that grants them tenure. New York State's policy requiring retirement at age 65 was also under consideration for change, raising the prospect that tenured faculty members would be allowed to work much longer.

In this climate transforming the organization was nearly impossible. The faculty and administration strongly resisted change of any kind. The status quo worked for them. Contractual constraints limited the flexibility to eliminate jobs.

Leslie, like chief executives in any sector, had two choices in this situation. He could make a command decision, in which a plan was devised, announced, and implemented by the top official, or he could take a more collaborative stance. That is, he could make a consultative, or consensus, decision, in which he sought employees' input and ideas in shaping the outcomes of the organization. In a command decision employees are simply expected to comply with the executive's goal and plans. It does not matter whether they agree or disagree. Their expertise or perspective is not taken into account; they must simply follow suit. In a collaborative decision the opposite is true. Here the employees are asked for their views and their recommendations about what to do in the first place or how to do something that is determined at the command level.

Leslie understood the importance of involving employees in a change of this kind. He was also convinced that the necessary healing would be expedited if survivors as well as those who left helped to shape the decision. In addition, one of his most pressing concerns was how to lead and implement the changes in a way that kept the self-esteem, morale, and competence of the survivors intact. He soon learned that this would be a challenging journey. As he explained,

> My first step was to develop a reorganization plan. I established several committees of faculty and administrators to advise me as to the best organizational structure and also to carry out a planning process in order to better define the new goals and objectives of the college. Privately, many faculty members told me change was needed. Officially, they resisted any change in the administration. The committees offered no recommendations. I was faced with having to develop the restructuring plan without official faculty input.

# RESTRUCTURING ONONDAGA COMMUNITY COLLEGE

Time being of the essence, Bruce Leslie decided to move forward with a plan. He had the support of the board, and with their input he mapped out the following strategic choices.

### *Establish a Long-Term Early Retirement Incentive*

An early retirement plan was accepted by the faculty union during negotiations in the spring of 1984. The program, which was modified in 1987 during subsequent contract negotiations, provided half pay to faculty members who had been at the institution for a minimum of ten years and had reached the age of fifty-five. With the passage later of legislation on age discrimination, a seventy-year-old faculty member could receive the early retirement incentive.

The college has been pressured by the county government to eliminate this overly generous entitlement program in the next round of collective bargaining. Nevertheless, the retirement incentive was Leslie's chief strategy to downsize OCC's workforce.

## *Plan and Respond to Community Needs*

Community colleges, as the name implies, have historically been rooted in a tradition of responding to local needs. When they first came on the scene in about 1960, they were a practical departure from the more "elite" two-year junior college, which prepared students for progression into a four-year baccalaureate program. In response to changing demographic and social needs, the community college's mission was to provide more open access to higher education. By focusing on job skills and providing the interim associate degree, the community college met the needs of a broader population of students seeking entry into the workforce at a technical level, as well as the needs of those who also wanted the flexibility of completing their higher education in incremental steps. Even today a significant number of students use the community college as preparation for transferring to a four-year baccalaureate degree program.

At the time these changes in education were taking place, local employers were swept up in the downsizing waves of the mid-1980s. Employers like Kodak and others in the area were laying off large numbers of employees or closing their doors altogether. The net effect was that OCC had the opportunity to serve an entirely new population: older displaced workers, many of whom were women or racial and ethnic minorities. The strategy of launching programs aimed at these groups was a sound one. Beyond the requirements of federal guidelines and OCC's policy of reflecting the demographic makeup of its community, Leslie also sought the benefits that come from diversity. In this spirit the college revamped its affirmative action programs, in the process establishing the Office of Multicultural Resources and Diversity Awareness. The net result of these changes was a growth in enrollment to more than eight thousand by 1993. OCC came to have the second largest disabled population in the state's university system, as well as a mix of students from a wide range of backgrounds.

With these developments have come other internal changes. The college has had to restructure its financial aid program and other support services, such as English as a second language, and has had to provide a professional staff to support the needs of students with disabilities. And there have been other issues to wrestle with as well. In Leslie's thinking,

> a healthy academic institution acknowledges that the world is changing and that students and faculty must be equipped to work on multicultural teams and lead and manage in a multicultural world. Curriculum and attitudes must constantly change to reflect this if the organization is to lead with integrity. Yet, downsizing and restructuring can compound diversity issues. As people of color leave, it would be nice to be able to maintain a healthy multicultural mix, but it is frustrating that positions cannot always be filled in a climate of cutbacks in ways that support that goal to everyone's satisfaction.

### Form Public-Private Sector Partnerships for Growth

In addition to meeting the growing needs of business and industry customers, the college has formed important partnerships with this sector. Its Community Education Center, for example, provided education and counseling to over 4,600 entrepreneurs, developed some 1,500 jobs, and generated over $30 million in investments between 1986 and 1993 through its Small Business Development Program. Ed Kowalski, director of workforce and business development at the center, works with individual companies to offer courses in areas such as leadership, teamwork, and problem solving. The Community Education Center thus acts as a profitable minibusiness within the college. Over ten years it grew from an initial staff of three people to twenty-two professionals, and it has served 25,000 students.

Kowalski offered the following observation about how this strategy has been received: "Bruce wants to bring OCC in line with supporting the business community. This strengthens the viability of the college, and that provides employment security for faculty and staff. Yet, he is both rapped and applauded for that depending on the values of the people you talk to."

## *Restructure Programs and Faculty and Staff Assignments*

Prior to Leslie's tenure, twenty-four academic and several administrative departments had reported to a single academic vice president, creating an unwieldy span of control. Faculty chairs functioned on the academic calendar, rendering them unavailable for five months a year. Several areas were overadministered, while others were underadministered. The structure was cumbersome, political, inefficient, and highly resistant to change. To restructure would require complicated collective bargaining changes in rank, program content, and staff support. It would also mean the elimination of certain program and job categories. Following an evaluation of costs and benefits against the new strategic goals, however, such changes were deemed necessary.

Leslie established three divisions, narrowing the span of control for greater efficiency. These were led by three deans reporting to the academic vice president. While this measure facilitated management of the substantial growth in student population, it was not entirely popular. The college was also restructured around four goals: academic development, student services, administrative efficiencies, and planning and technology advancement.

Although in some cases the efforts to renegotiate faculty loads failed, there were many adjustments made. For example, the faculty rank of instructor's assistant had previously been assigned to lab support duty, a nonfaculty-level job. This was changed through attrition to the position of technical assistant, a civil service rank at lower pay. Similar adjustments were made in the nursing department, where a faculty member was reassigned from the level of professor to the level of instructor assistant. Many faculty members were also reassigned from obsolete disciplines to other departments and disciplines in which they had teaching skills. For example, by eliminating the ensemble approach in the music department, the number of full-time faculty required diminished. Two music department faculty members were moved to the business department. One was a piano instructor who was also an attorney capable of teaching business law. The other, a former woodwind instructor and computer expert, moved to teach computer courses in the business program.

Central to this strategy was Leslie's commitment to retraining survivors. In cases of reassignment, faculty members were given sabbaticals if they wanted them to "retool and retrain themselves." Several faculty members took advantage of this benefit. One moved from anthropology to sociology; another moved from medical technology to biology. In fact, in one case the surviving employee was provided additional study leave outside the faculty sabbatical process. As one faculty member described it to me, "Bruce did everything he could after my program was axed. He gave me time off to try to get my act together. I hadn't had a biology course since 1950. I had to get back into shape again, so to speak. I got a sabbatical to help me go back and retrain and take those courses again. I have no complaints with how he handled the changes. . . . He bent over backwards. . . . He was extremely generous." Then she added an observation that reminds us of the survivor's syndrome in any case, "It's just frustrating when your identity is taken from you."

—

None of this was lost on Leslie. Being well versed in an appreciation of organizational dynamics, he understood only too well that, in choosing to move ahead with his restructuring plans, the symptoms of resistance to change would erupt into full-blown survivor syndrome. And so it did. When I first met with the Onondaga administration and faculty, they had moved past shock and denial into various stages of anger, tinged with the beginnings of an uneasy acceptance.

"I don't go to faculty meetings anymore," said a long-term instructor speaking of a restructuring move that had altered the nature of her job, "because I have been listening to the same people shoot off their mouths for over twenty-five years. I just stick with my students and that is it. . . . I guess I'm still very angry over the whole thing." To this a colleague, another long-term faculty member, added, "It all comes back to communication, I think. They should have come to you to discuss what they were going to do. Given their rationale, you would have had the opportunity to give your reasons why you should keep doing things as you were doing them." The first faculty member then grudgingly conceded, "Well, in fact they did talk to me, and we did discuss the pros and cons and cost effectiveness . . . in all fairness to them."

Members of the senior administration were open and honest in talking about their experiences as survivor leaders. "Exciting," "challenging," "a little scary," and "sometimes frustrating" were among the adjectives they used to describe the restructuring environment under Leslie. As one director put it, "Change is always scary. We're at an exciting time with all kinds of new things, but success is not assured. So, we are at least employed at the campus at a significant time in its development."

Another senior administrator spoke about the inevitable loss of confidence and competence that so often accompanies restructuring:

I am feeling less confident in my abilities. Within the last year I took on a new department. It is a learning curve that is longer

than I would have liked. I am feeling my way so I am less secure in my own ability. It will return, I think, in time, but I am
not really sure yet if the new structure is correct or that we have
made the last change. Over time I will know more, understand
more, and have a few successes in the new structure. . . . I think
right now we are all in transition.

While employees expressed concern about clarifying the
college's vision and direction and about getting everyone to see
the big picture from the perspective of the students' needs,
they conceded that in downsizing and restructuring they were
in fact moving in the right direction. "I don't think we are the
archetype . . . of how to heal the downsized organization," offered one of the deans, "but I think we have done a pretty good
job in terms of supporting those people who were most se-
verely affected. I inherited an employee who was affected. I
was also a person who participated in the layoff of an administrator. . . . We are best represented as a 'work in progress.' You
could say we had some successes and learned some things."

## LESSONS FROM ONONDAGA
## COMMUNITY COLLEGE

The story of Onondaga Community College reminds us that
change does not unfold in a predictable, linear fashion and
that contemporary models of collaborative decision making
must at times be tempered with the courage to make tough
command decisions in a crisis. It raises the issue of managerial
decision making in the face of downsizing and restructuring. It
also reminds us that survivor needs are shaped by the cultural
context of the organization, further supporting the idea that to
heal downsizing, restructuring organizations in any sector
managers must develop expertise in planning cultural change.
    The following tactical leadership choices have contributed
much to the healing taking place at OCC. According to Bruce
Leslie, these healing strategies have begun to discourage people from trying to circle the wagon to protect what is familiar.

## *Retain and Retrain Whenever Possible*

Bruce Leslie decided that for his restructuring plan to be considered a success it had to do more than simply reduce overhead costs. His definition of success had an even more important human dimension. He would offer all assistance possible to those who had to leave, while attempting to retain staff members whenever possible. He would implement downsizing and restructuring measures in a way that preserved the competence, viability, and self-esteem both of those who left and those who remained. In his words, "Philosophically I believe people's jobs are critical to their sense of self. It is their livelihood; it is central to their family and to their community. Our vision talks about transforming the community and preparing the workforce of the future. How can I conduct lay-offs without careful attention to both the needs of those who leave and the needs of those who remain?"

One example of this commitment could be seen when the decision was made to eliminate the word-processing department, which was run by two women. Like organizations everywhere, the community college had evolved to the point where most people had the capacity to do their own word processing at their desks. Eliminating the traditional word-processing department would cut costs, even if it did meet with the expected resistance from those who now had to take care of their own word-processing needs. In eliminating the department, extreme care was taken to ensure that the two women would be survivors rather than casualties of the department cut. They were reassigned elsewhere, like the biology and music teachers in the examples cited earlier, sending the clear message to the rest of the college community that pains were being taken across the board to retain people whenever possible.

Plans also were made to get more expertise in the computer area to keep the college abreast of technological advances. Again, the strategy was to identify people internally who had an interest in computing and to give them the necessary retraining.

Leslie firmly believes that sending this message about a commitment to retain and retrain is central to survivor security and healing as the college faces necessary uncertainties and changes. He feels that this not only serves to rebuild morale but also continues to add value to the college. Thus, another round of such retraining has been scheduled: "We have areas where we need people with different skills; rather than go outside to fill these positions, my plan is to tap our existing faculty and staff. They are good people—motivated, dedicated, and highly retrainable."

## Don't Sacrifice Quality for Efficiency

Under Leslie's leadership, a movement has developed at OCC, as in many forward thinking colleges, to define measurements, benchmarks, and other indexes for student success. The goal is to identify clear, observable measures of progress, along with methods for moving from the present state to where students ought to be in the future. This approach enables the faculty and administration to talk in concrete terms for the first time about what steps to take to achieve goals, how long it will take, and so forth. Equally important, in a climate in which downsizing is the norm and funding is scarce, it positions the college to be more competitive when talking to politicians and funding sources about its needs and about the consequences if funding isn't available. Among the emerging quality standards is a commitment to maintaining a 60 percent permanent faculty, which is above the national norm. Asked why this choice was made, Leslie explains, "You can't compromise quality because you are cutting costs. We need a critical mass of full-time faculty for planning, advising, and counseling in order to ensure excellence and the viability of the college. It's not just about their teaching load."

In keeping with this stance, Leslie does not believe in mechanical, across-the-board formulas for cuts of the sort often used in industry. Instead, he carefully looks at each case, each academic program area, and attempts to maintain healthy faculty-to-students ratios. He takes into account all the quality measures in assessing how to make cuts. While people account for 85 percent of his budget, Leslie does not see people as costs to be cut. He acknowledges that this approach may mean that it might take years to accomplish his goals, but he feels that the payoffs for survivors and higher morale levels make it worth the time.

## *Plan and Respond to Both the Internal and External Environments*

A loss of identity was a major restraining force against change for the survivors at Onondaga Community College. As a rule, faculty members have chosen academia because it is not corporate, allows intellectual freedom, and in a sense enables those with an autonomous bent to be their own bosses. The academic sector, however, now faces new threats to the coveted security of tenure for life and the pursuit of intellectual independence. But many academic survivors remain in hopeless denial about the need to change. They comfortably reside in disenchantment, disillusionment, and blame when their position is challenged. Leslie recalled a conversation in which, after having viewed a television documentary on Internet University and its foray into electronic education, he asked a faculty member, "How will we respond to this? It will potentially affect our enrollment, our integrity, our offerings." The faculty member suggested that the college promote itself as an institution that vigorously protects tradition and upholds timeless academic values in the face of sweeping changes.

This conversation is an important reminder of the loss of identity to the survivors of any change. A restructuring such as that at OCC means a totally new academic culture driven by technology, the needs of external customers, and other forces. A balanced attention to both internal customers (employees) and external customers (students, government, business, and so forth) is key to leading and managing survivors so as to re-create a more viable organization. Leslie describes his position as follows:

> Universities are here to respond to the need of the entire community. We cannot afford to allow the ivory tower to take over. We can't be all things to all people, but we must be in touch with the needs of business, social service providers, political leaders, and the needs of our faculty and staff. This is how we keep our finger on the pulse of what's important. This allows us to make the right decisions about our programs and what we offer. Academics take umbrage at the phrase "customer driven" because many don't like business terms and our culture has traditionally been suspicious of business. I try to educate people to think about the business world and about the business of running their own classroom as well. What are the skills we must have to prepare students to be successful in the global economy? What are the outcomes that students will have to demonstrate at the end of two years with us? Now that my faculty have acknowledged that this is important, I have engaged them in taking the lead in posing these questions to the community.

## Ride the Wave of Technology

Technology is permeating everything at Onondaga Community College. Plans have been made for the building of a Center for Business, Industry, and Technology. The center is to provide state-of-the-art education in areas such as electronics, mechanical technology, radio, and television. Leslie's goal is to stay on the leading edge in preparing students for the workplace of tomorrow and in preparing teachers to teach in the classroom of the future. The technology center is to be a model of what the rest of the college eventually should look like.

The message for survivors is clear. Faculty members must

become comfortable with technology if the college and their future are to remain viable. Leslie feels that each full-time faculty member should have a personal computer, yet he is aware of resistance to this idea in the form of faculty comments that the students, not the instructors, should be given the computers. There is trepidation from some faculty members who don't want to see technology change the familiar classrooms they have known for ages. Leslie is concerned about finding stimulating and supportive ways to move such faculty members away from "teaching the way they were taught in school."

Leslie understands that there is no quick fix, but by engaging people through technology he hopes to stimulate and support a new kind of creativity. He calls it "creating momentum for change in a positive way." This time around he is taking a more patient, soft-sell approach in dealing with survivor resistance to change, without wavering in his conviction that this is the right leadership choice. Recognizing that these goals will generate another round of faculty retraining, he has set up a faculty committee to lead this transition. The committee has begun to hold a range of elective training programs for the faculty, and there is a growing interest in and comfort with these courses. As Leslie explains, "The lesson I've learned is that faculty can't be force-fed. The Faculty Computing Committee training works because people are invited to apply for computers and training, rather than being mandated to do so. It's also modeling the way in a nonthreatening fashion."

*Convene Formal Forums for Change*

Leslie, aware of a pressing need to engage survivors in a collaborative effort at shaping the future of Onondaga Community College and reducing resistance to change, engaged the services of management consultant Mary Gail Biebel to lead a planned change and team-building process. As he put it,

> I wanted to educate and involve more people in faculty and administrative leadership so they would have firsthand knowl-

edge of the exigencies we were dealing with. In the past I would tell them in meetings about the need to restructure and manage costs. They heard but they didn't internalize the message, and the loud critics didn't show up. When they are involved firsthand, they understand how it is. I also want to encourage people to vent. I make every effort to personally talk with faculty and staff who need to complain and release their feelings about loss. I want people to have a sense of security— no fear of losing their jobs because they speak their piece.

Leslie's decision to launch a collaborative decision-making process for budgeting fortuitously also became the rallying point around which an important group of decision makers began to coalesce for the first time. In an unprecedented move, every faculty and staff member who had budgeting or line responsibility for functional areas was invited to become part of this interdisciplinary budgeting team. The team included deans, faculty members, coordinators, and the heads of such functional areas as security and maintenance. It also provided a much needed opportunity to educate everyone on the process, challenges, and political constraints of budgeting at the same time that it empowered them to shape the future of their institution. Sixty to eighty OCC decision makers have been involved in a series of extended planning, leadership, and team-building meetings that encompass everything from training in trust building and dealing with style differences to allocating dollars and managing change.

According to Biebel this has been a significant process for healing in the face of change because "it was something that was timely, cut across various constituents, and had enough of a 'hook' to capture people's attention and engage them in influencing outcomes. It was also a kind of a test case—an exercise in trust building through collaborative decision making and challenging each other to move forward with this."

Referring to William Bridges's transition and change model, Biebel described two camps that created real conflict and chaos at the initial stages of her work with the budget planning team: those firmly ensconced in holding on to the old ways of doing things, and those firmly planted in the new camp. She described her struggles with leading these academic survivors from letting go to accepting change in the following way:

> Academia by the way it's set up is rooted in job security. It's an institution that hasn't changed a lot. It's not like the joy of working in a fast-paced, rapidly growing high-tech organization where when you talk about change it's routine for them, they immediately get it. But I see how difficult it is for these people, many of whom have spent their whole life in the organization, to embrace these changes. I think that Bruce went out of his way to restructure jobs and reeducate people, yet people didn't take advantage. They were so much in denial.

> They also misdiagnose the limits of their leader's influence. Traditionally provosts and presidents in academic organizations had a great deal of power that they no longer have—the power of money and making decisions. Now they are much more business managers. Bruce's job is getting funding, moving his organization forward, fighting political battles as he tries to reposition his organization for the future, and I think these people try to credit him with powers and abilities that he doesn't have so they are disappointed often. They get caught in a parent-child thing where they are dependent on him, yet paradoxically they want to be very autonomous. . . .

Some participants credit Biebel's work with the budget team for moving the faculty and staff away from denial, anger, and resistance toward bargaining and acceptance of change. She has done this by using the following strategies designed to "move participants from surviving to thriving":

- providing a structured, supportive framework for team members to discuss budget matters and work on relationships and trust building;
- establishing benchmarks and milestones for gauging changes and acknowledging successes;

- helping participants to understand the process and nature of change and the basis for survivor behavior such as blaming the initiator of the change or holding on to what is familiar;
- providing skill building in leadership, management, quality training, dealing with style differences and conflict, and active listening;
- serving as a sounding board and providing "reality checks," like eliciting what people might be feeling and comparing it to their counterparts in other organizations, assuring them that "you're not alone; this is normal";
- giving team members "permission" and opportunities to express their feelings.

"They say I give them hope," Biebel confides, "by assuring them that if they keep going down this path they will get through the transition, to the new beginning."

Asked about his future plans for the continued healing of his restructuring organization, Bruce Leslie offered four simple goals:

- Keep people directed toward affirming opportunities for growth and positive contributions.
- Give people even more opportunities to be involved.
- Create a supportive environment in which people are not gripped by the fear of losing their jobs because they speak their piece.
- Remind everyone that we are all in this together.

## SUMMARY OF LESSONS FROM ONONDAGA COMMUNITY COLLEGE

- Retain and retrain whenever possible.
- Don't sacrifice quality for efficiency.

- Plan and respond to both the internal and external environments. Be customer driven.
- Ride the wave of technology as a rallying point for change.
- Convene formal forums for change.

# Chapter 7

—m—

# THE GENERAL ELECTRIC
# APPLIANCES CASE

We had been labeled Strike City, USA. When things were good, they kicked us; when things were bad, we kicked them. I felt we should move from being enemies to becoming partners. We all want good jobs to support our families. We all want the same things. So labor and management sat down and worked out our differences so everyone could get their needs met. It took hard work and players on both sides, but it was the right thing to do.

These are the words of Norm Mitchell, president of the International Union of Electronic, Electrical, Salaried, Machine and Furniture Workers, AFL-CIO (IUE) Local 761 in Louisville, Kentucky. Mitchell, a General Electric employee since August 1953, has held every union office during his twenty-seven years in the labor movement. He was thrust into the limelight as head of the union when the former president became ill. Little did he know that the office would plunge him into the midst of a revolution in business, requiring him to exercise exemplary leadership as part of a labor-management alliance designed to save GE's Appliance Park.

Throughout this book I have written about the pain of survivor syndrome—the loss of trust, the frustration, the anger and anxiety, the feeling of disempowerment. I could very well have been writing about the mood of America's labor-management scene. The very existence of labor unions has to do with the fears and concerns voiced by today's survivors: Do they have our best interests at heart? Do they know what they're doing? Will they act with honesty and integrity in their dealings with us? These are the questions that, when answered in the negative, lead to distrust. These are the questions voiced by downsizing survivors and survivor managers. They are also the questions that have been voiced by labor and management in every sector for decades. These questions of trust are often answered in the negative, leading to the uneasy relationships between those in power and those who seek more power in the workplace.

The crises of downsizing and the restructuring activities of the eighties and nineties have forced labor and management to confront these issues of trust more squarely. There is agreement in both camps that joint labor-management participation and collaboration may well be a critical path to healing the wounds of the past and to resolving the threats to our economic future. But the rhetoric has far outpaced the behavior. In most cases the distrust between both groups continues, and promises on both parts often fade behind fickle commitments.

The GE Appliances story is about healing the labor-management rift as a business revitalizes itself in the face of harsh economic realities. It describes conditions that are rarely discussed in the literature on downsizing and restructuring but that must be resolved to achieve organizational renewal in the nineties.

General Electric (GE) is one of America's best-known and most-admired companies. This $70 billion global company employs 265,000 employees and is often touted as being the world's largest exporter of manufactured goods and services. The company's extensive business portfolio includes aircraft and medical technology, plastics, financial services, media, and such varied products as transportation systems, lightbulbs, electric motors, and appliances. In the years following World War II, GE, like many big companies of that era, experienced steady growth for decades as it divested, made acquisitions, embraced new technology, and modeled the way through impressive business maneuvers.

GE's accomplishments have been led by a long line of visionary, powerful homegrown leaders. Gerard Swope, CEO from 1922 to 1939, led the company into the home appliances business, which is the subject of this story. He is credited with introducing the concept of "enlightened management," which was designed to distribute responsibility equally among employees, shareholders, and customers. Ralph Cordiner, CEO from 1950 to 1963, was equally celebrated for his contribution to management as he aggressively moved GE into a series of new businesses, established its now famous Crotonville, New York, management training center, and introduced the then popular concept of management by objective as he rallied employees under the slogan "Go for it." Reginald Jones, CEO from 1973 to 1980, grew GE's pretax profits at unprecedented rates and, in surveys conducted by *U.S. News & World Report*, *The Wall Street Journal*, and *Fortune* magazine, was dubbed by his peers "the most admired business leader in America" and "the most influential person in business today."

When Jack Welch became CEO in 1981, he took his place among his predecessors very naturally. He immediately became, and has remained, the subject of business journals, business school cases, and corporate management seminars. He was described in the December 13, 1993, issue of *Fortune* as "the leading master of corporate change in our time" ("A Master Class in Radical Change"). His commitment to unleashing the power of employees' ideas and skills is legendary and defines much of what is taught in GE's comprehensive training programs. As Welch sees it, "The idea of liberation and empowerment for our work force is not enlightenment—it's a competitive necessity" ("The Mind of Jack Welch," *Fortune*, March 27, 1989, 46).

At the same time it is clear that Welch's vision is to foster sweeping transformational change. Internally he expects to create an organizational culture that supports teams first and that uses joint problem solving at all levels to improve efficiency and productivity as workers jointly create a revitalized, more competitive organization. He has made great strides to create an organization that is based on open communication, effective leadership, and interpersonal relations at all levels. He has sponsored and supported employee movements to ensure that GE is an organization which values the diverse makeup, backgrounds, and ideas of all its employees and in which relationships are based on mutual trust and respect.

But through all these internal changes and activities, GE is expected not to lose sight of its primary goal. The commitment to revitalizing the way people work together and the way the business is run is designed to achieve an unparalleled commitment to customer satisfaction. Welch is often quoted as saying, "Companies can't give job security. Only customers can." This communicates a very clear message: people's survival depends on their ability to generate bottom line results gained through customer satisfaction.

Welch's visionary leadership has paid off. In 1991 *Fortune* magazine lauded GE as one of the eight most innovative companies in America. In 1994 *Fortune* ranked GE as number 14 among 395 of "America's Most Admired Corporations." The rating was based on eight attributes: quality of management; quality of product or services; innovativeness; long-term investment value; financial soundness; ability to attract, develop, and keep talented people; responsibility to the community and environment; and wise use of corporate assets.

But none of this has inoculated GE from the economic ailments of the past two decades. Like companies everywhere, GE has had to face the challenge of rejuvenating its business practices in order to continue to survive and prosper in an environment made severe by stiff global competition. This was compounded by a management culture that had begun to lead to internal lethargy and inhibited continued revenue growth. Such was the challenge Welch faced when, in 1981, after twenty-one years with the company in which he had worked his way up from engineer to vice president, he became chairman and CEO.

Caught in the sweeping economic changes of the eighties and nineties, Welch has led the downsizing and reorganization of the entire corporation. He has stripped away layers of management, from nine levels to as few as four in some areas. He has divested businesses with over 170,000 employees, decreasing the workforce from around 400,000 in 1981 to 265,000 fifteen years later. Welch frequently makes presentations at the company's Crotonville Management Development Institute and regularly visits GE factories, spreading the word about the necessary changes and the values and behavior expected in the new GE culture.

GE Appliances, a business unit established in 1953, is one of the largest manufacturers of major appliances in the world. It generates 10 percent of General Electric's revenues and accounts for roughly $6 billion in sales annually. Headquartered in Louisville in its impressive 1,200-acre Appliance Park facility, GE Appliances supplies 150 world markets with such products as refrigerators, electric and gas ranges, dishwashers, microwave ovens, washers, dryers, and room air conditioners. As the largest manufacturing site owned by General Electric, GE Appliances employs 7,000 union workers.

In 1988 GE Appliances faced a crisis that could easily have led to its obsolescence. Appliance Park had become inefficient and continued to lose money. To compound matters further, GE Appliances was besieged by a history of adversarial labor relations, resulting in what the company describes as the "four Ss": strikes, sabotage, subterfuge, slowdowns. Appliance Park, with an extremely high incidence of grievances, unacceptable quality standards, counterproductive work practices, and extreme distrust and tension between labor and management, was poised on the brink of failure. Rather than focusing their energies on fighting external competitors like Whirlpool, GE employees and management were inwardly focused, fighting one another.

Things came to a head in 1992 when the laundry business at Appliance Park set out to produce a new washing machine design that featured an integrated tub and basket. Plans for the new washer went off track, and GE's marketing people, sensing a problem, looked outside to see if competitors would "outsource" GE's laundry products. This meant that appliances such as the washing machine would be developed through joint ventures whereby another company manufactured them under the GE name. According to Bill McDonogh, manager of the Department of Human Resources, Manufacturing, Purchasing, and Quality, "We were on the verge of losing our laundry line. If we couldn't pull this off, it would have led to our demise over time."

At the corporate level all of this translated into a lack of confidence in Appliance Park's ability to transform itself sufficiently to survive. It was clear from the beginning that Welch's single agenda was to revolutionize a business that was going from being a robust industry leader to one that could suffocate on its bureaucratic excesses and sluggish performance. Welch took a tough position toward all GE businesses. His message was clear: demonstrate that you can strengthen your weak business or go out of business. Specifically, Welch's agenda was that activities at General Electric must be fired by the single vision: to make GE number one or two in all of its businesses. If a business cannot achieve this, it must be fixed, sold, or closed. This was viewed as a competitive must—necessary for the company's survival. Appliance Park, facing serious labor-management problems and recognizing Welch's lack of faith in its ability to renew itself, was plunged into a major crisis.

In union president Mitchell's words,

As I toured the country to attend different meetings, I heard the words "merger," "buyout," "consolidation," "Mexico," "China." I learned of the closing of our room air conditioner business—sold to the Japanese. That was devastating. Heretofore it was always somebody else. Now it was us. This was around 1986. As the reality of the changes hit home for us, it seemed like there was nothing we could do or say. But when I saw what was happening across the U.S., I realized there was no longer peace of mind for workers anywhere. I had security because of seniority, but I became really concerned about the workers I represent. I decided I had to go and talk to the CEO, Jack Welch. I told the company that the next time he came to Louisville I wanted to talk to him. My wife asked me, "Are you nervous?" I said, "No. He's a man just like me; we all want the same for our families." When I met with him, he asked me what was on my mind, and I told him: "What can we do, within reason, to support our people and keep making appliances in Louisville, Kentucky?"

The union president's willingness to forge a collaborative relationship based on honest communications, the CEO's commitment to forging change by unleashing the human power of the workforce, and the buy-in and strong leadership of the Appliance Park management team all became a winning combination for transformational change.

Skeeter Cole, manager of labor relations at Appliance Park, recalls the crisis and its resolution:

We all recognized that we had become too inefficient. If we didn't show productivity improvement, the corporation would no longer invest in Appliance Park. Plant management met with the union to share concerns about this. There were no holds barred. We got together in a room and started writing ideas on the wall. We came up with two hundred to three hundred ideas [and] whittled them down to forty-three initiatives designed to make Appliance Park work. We had been slowly working toward employee involvement across all of our operations all along, but this crisis, the corporate decision to eliminate Appliance Park, became the rallying point. Norm Mitchell's leadership was good. Prior to 1988 this was strike city. We have not had a strike over a grievance since we decided to "Save the Park."

"Save the Park" became the rallying cry for GE Appliances as labor and management came together in an unprecedented effort to rescue the business. The "Save the Park" joint labor-management committee formed in December 1992 used the famous GE problem-solving process called Work-Out to reach agreements and generate plans for Appliance Park's future.

The idea of creating a revolution from within at Appliance Park was consistent with corporate expectations. But it was not an easy road to take. In the appliance business the operational margins are thin. A company cannot pass costs on to customers in this market, and so it must make money through productivity improvements and by generating large enough volumes to compete successfully. This means cutting costs and getting a lot more out of people. So, there were layoffs to contend with as the "Save the Park" efforts got under way. Employee morale suffered as workers confronted their losses and the numerous changes they had to live through. The new labor-management relationship was a hard sell both for union members and managers. As Mitchell explains,

> There were those who criticized me and said I was in bed with the company. Yes, it's a partnership—somewhat like a marriage. Marriages fail if you stop talking. The stands I took were not popular. My whole executive board turned against me at one point because I was making too many changes. It was unprecedented, but I won with a whole new slate. It's like the change to color television. People resisted simply because it was different. There will be no future without change.

Cole told a similar story from the management perspective:

> The transition is more difficult for management in many ways. We have to give up power when we give more decision-making responsibility to the union. Some managers have a problem with that. They are not used to it. So we train supervisors and managers in making this transition. We train them to be sounding boards rather than just supervisors. We train them how to work with teams and manage changes.

But because of the impressive labor-management dialogue, joint problem solving in Work-Out sessions, retraining and retooling of employees, and opportunities to rise to the challenge of saving their business, the layoffs and other cost-cutting measures were handled as humanely as possible. In the meantime labor and management, by putting their heads together, engaged survivors in saving the business. Together they set a $60 million productivity target. They analyzed every cost and came up with forty-three initiatives, including everything from total teamwork to increasing training. They took two of their buildings apart and installed new world-class assembly lines. They came to enjoy record-breaking schedule achievements daily, significantly improved quality, and realized over $58 million in productivity gains in the first two years.

Doug Wichmann is a plant manager at Appliance Park. His unit was not directly involved in the cuts, but, like others at Appliance Park, he was closely aware of the challenges and the changes. His plant manufactures dishwashers, a pretty competitive, growing business with a stabilized workforce of about 1,625 employees. As Wichmann sees it, customers and survivors must be supported through the process if the organization's health is to be restored after downsizing:

> Downsizing and restructuring are unfortunate, but necessary activities in today's workplace. Our doom would be sealed if we didn't do it. But we also have a responsibility to our customers and employees to make things work for them. In the appliance industry we could have easily moved overseas—we want to keep the major percentage of the jobs here in the U.S. to protect our workers' interests. So we have to downsize, then grow, improve market share, bring people back if possible, and forge ahead. We used early retirements to minimize the impact of downsizing. Survivors that are near retirement see that taking the attractive packages might help others save their jobs. It has been a real win-win outcome for us. We encourage it without forcing it. So although we have less numbers overall, we have

done a good job of preserving and supporting people as we deal with the necessary evil of cutting jobs today.

This joint venture is working to heal and revitalize labor-management relationships at Appliance Park and in the GE Appliances business. A symbolic tribute to the commitment behind this new labor-management alliance is the new logo and slogan. The design has two gears facing each other and the words "GE and IUE Partners in Progress Geared for the Future."

In November 1995 just three years after "Save the Park" was launched, GE Appliances received the Work in America Institute Leadership Award "in recognition of the cooperative spirit that unites labor and management."

## LESSONS FROM GENERAL ELECTRIC APPLIANCES

### *The Workforce Can Be Partners in Change*

At GE the liberation and empowerment of the workforce meant creating a new culture in which work teams were expected to be full partners in identifying and resolving business problems at all levels. According to Doug Wichmann, "Our employees now see their role in shaping the future of their business. And they are making great strides because they are involved. If you get people thinking and sharing their ideas, it's remarkable what you can do."

One mechanism for this approach to running the business is the GE Work-Out, which involves employees in a process of shared leadership. Work-Outs started out as town meetings with a facilitator and a cross section of people from all levels of the organization getting together in intensive brainstorming sessions to explore problems and generate suggested solutions.

The results from these meetings are disseminated to appropriate "sponsoring" managers and the union leadership through a Report Out session. Everyone must agree on a proposed project for it to fly. There are three possible outcomes of a Report Out session: (1) the leadership disagrees, in which case the idea dies; (2) the leadership requests more studies or further consideration; or (3) the proposal is approved and given the necessary support and resources by the sponsoring manager to enable it to be implemented.

Work-Outs are about people listening to one another, allowing them to air their views, surface innovative ideas, and collaborate as teams to make those ideas come to fruition. This approach to teamwork has not only contributed to quality improvement at Appliance Park, but it also has become a major process of empowerment that contributes in a major way to healing the pangs of loss and change in its various plants.

Initially Work-Out sessions involved only salaried employees helping the management team. Seizing its crisis as a catalyst for further change, Appliance Park took the Work-Out process to the plant floor. Each building took a separate topic, such as reducing waste, and worked it through until an effective solution was agreed upon and implemented. Plant management, supervisors, and employees began to work together to generate cost savings, safety improvements, productivity gains, award programs, and so forth.

An important aspect of the Work-Out process was the training of facilitators at all levels. According to human resources manager Bill McDonogh, some of the best facilitators were from the shop. Each building at Appliance Park has a group of trained facilitators who can run a session at any time.

GE Appliances now conducts 95 percent of its activities through work teams—a natural evolution of the Work-Out process. Some of these teams are self-directed, further supporting the businesses goals of empowering survivors to lead change. This healthy, collaborative process between labor and management is an important cultural change for GE Appliances. Management and the union view it as an educational process in which both hourly and salaried workers learn more about the business and its constraints and are challenged and stimulated by the prospect of helping to ensure their future and the future of the business.

What it boils down to, says Norm Mitchell, is that management is finally getting the message: "Start listening to the American worker. They are the smartest people in the world. Jack Welch is to be given credit for starting to use workers' brain power."

Today there is good evidence that this value is being reflected in day-to-day business choices. Survivors are informed the minute a change is decided upon and are given the opportunity to figure ways to make it work. They are also notified whenever a decision is made to outsource something. Employees are then given six months to get their costs in line, effectively to become the "vendor of choice" competing internally with the external source. Management's promise to the workforce is that "If you demonstrate that you can compete with the vendors' quotes, we'll keep the business here." Recently, for example, a decision was made to outsource the manufacturing of dishwasher racks to external vendors who could produce them for less. The wire rack people responded and beat the vendors—putting one out of business.

Another example of this subtle movement toward the "self-employed employee" was found in operations in Building 5A. This Appliance Park facility makes plastic parts for refrigeration. The costs had risen higher than outside vendors, it employed 180 people, and it was not competitive. When plans for a shutdown were announced, employees were given six months to turn things around before outsourcing would begin. The operation survived. The facility now has forty employees, the output is greater, and the costs are lower than two years ago. Says Mitchell, "This is a fair way to treat people. Sometimes they make it, sometimes they don't, but they feel a bit more confidence because of this opportunity to protect their jobs."

## *Labor-Management Dialogue Must Radically Change*

A key to moving from surviving to thriving has been the major shift to more communication up front on the state of the business and more honest dialogue between the hourly and salaried workforce at GE Appliances. There are now work team meetings with hourly employees for a half hour every week in which they are kept posted on the competition and how well the company is doing. These meetings have become important forums for disseminating information and getting feedback, and all employees participate in them. Hourly coordinators run the meetings, along with salaried partners called "coaches." The coach serves as a sounding board and resource person who can resolve employee issues.

The plants have also instituted periodic roundtable meetings in which union leadership and management share information about business and industry issues. In addition, ongoing informal communication is strongly sanctioned. Supervisors are encouraged and retrained to walk the floor and listen to people. As Doug Wichmann explained, "They see we are visible and that we care—we talk informally, we listen to each other, so it's a team initiative all around. The more informed people are, the more motivated they are to perform better, significantly reducing the risk of future downsizing. If you don't keep survivors informed until there is a problem, it really damages morale."

A part of the key to engaging and supporting survivors is telling them the full truth. The feeling at Appliance Park is that the hourly workforce can and should be expected to handle full information about business realities. Not only does this engender more respect for both parties, but it is also central to creating ownership in the business. Norm Mitchell says, "We were up front with people about the layoffs. We explained that if the economy turns down and people are not buying there will be less work. We also made it clear to them that layoffs are not their fault. It's also partly due to corporate greed in America and other economic problems."

There is now less need for the formal Work-Outs of the past because the process, the thinking, and the high level of communication are done as a routine part of the way labor-management teams function.

## *Invest in the Labor Force*

In planning for the future of current employees, the Appliance Park management has taken measures to improve the quality of the work life for survivors. This includes better lighting, better equipment, and other investments in the facility. As one manager explained, "We cannot forget that our employees are our future. New processes, new jobs, a nice setup, and air-conditioned facilities help to ease the pain of changes and make people feel more valued and better about coming to work."

As the organization continues to heal itself in the aftermath of its challenges, matters of worker relations are given much importance. GE Appliances is mindful of our increasingly family-centered work culture. For example, the needs of its summer workforce, as employees take vacations, are met in an innovative way that sends the message to survivors that the company cares. The sons and daughters of employees are given the opportunity to cover for lost time during vacations. Some of them later became full-time employees at Appliance Park.

Training is also high on the agenda at GE Appliances, as it is throughout the rest of the corporation. The plans for training are well thought out and proactive—aimed at increasing employees' competence and confidence in their work as it positions the business to be more competitive. The goal is to provide a broad training spectrum that covers technical and human skills equally. There are fifty-two hours of preemployment training, for example, and team leader training for supervisors in all buildings to equip them for the new team-oriented culture and the challenges of managing in a downsizing, restructuring environment. New hires go through work team training for several weeks, followed by refresher training. In addition, the specialized training conducted in the maintenance and tool and die areas are state of the art. Tuition reimbursement for college degrees and assistance in earning a high school equivalency diploma are accessible to all, and GE's state-assisted apprentice program is an industry model.

Norm Mitchell expresses the union's view about investing in survivors for the future in this way:

> We have [a] social responsibility to employees. Corporate America must care about its workers; then we will go the extra mile to be competitive. This applies equally to those who are let go and those who stay. In handling the layoffs we had to hire a full-time person to help people with their résumés. Some workers don't have the skills to even do that themselves. Corporations make gigantic bucks because of their workers. I challenge the company to look for new ways to support and reward them. We work together to find ways to cut costs and improve efficiency without cutting people and damaging their morale and their future.

> This is a social responsibility that big business has. Young people today are disturbed because America has not been able to give them peace of mind. How can we tell kids not to hang out at the corner when their daddies are being laid off?

> I ran into a salaried worker this morning who was frustrated. She needed to take the baby to the hospital but couldn't come up with the 50 percent because of her primary care arrangement. She had to pick the sick child up at the day care, she was frustrated, this will affect her job performance, so it's partly the company's responsibility to assist her in getting her needs met.

> And workers also have a responsibility to invest in themselves. Workers should learn computers, for example. If I were younger, I would find out as much about computers as I could. You'll get left behind these days if you don't learn this. I speak in the high schools, and I tell young people you can never get too much education. Think, think, think. This is why the union is a strong advocate of education. We just recently started a joint apprentice training program. It's a four-year pro-

gram that includes GED and computer training. We have graduations to celebrate and everything. Anyone can request this training, and they are encouraged. You can never get too much education.

### *Encourage Truth Telling as the Basis of Trust Building*

Perhaps the biggest gain in GE Appliances has been the leap of faith in opening up labor-management communications to allow employees at all levels to engage in honest, open dialogue and in problem solving with one another. While the typical uneasiness and morale issues associated with change still need to be worked on, it is clear that people sense they have more of a voice in shaping their company's (and by implication their own) future. As Norm Mitchell put it,

> I preach three words: trust, respect, and communication. You take any one of the three out and we cannot have a successful working relationship between hourly workers and management. We encourage people in our joint roundtable meetings to speak up. They can challenge anyone—you have the whole executive board with plant managers, schedulers, workers, everyone sitting at the same table telling it like they see it.

> It's all based on trust. The people had enough faith and trust to keep me around for twenty-eight years. I had the opportunity to serve and to leave a mark on the company. I have helped GE employees as well as others. Chrysler has taken our ideas and built on them, doing it even better than we are on such matters as the team concepts. Groups visit, and we give them advice.

Human Resources manager Bill McDonogh gives other examples that indicate how open communication and trust building are affecting the way work gets done as traditional organizational boundaries break down and methods of doing things more efficiently and effectively are found:

Each RIF (reduction-in-force) reverberates through the buildings because of bumping from jobs due to seniority. We worked together to take a lot of steps out of the bumps and simplified things. We run a bump in a day instead of two weeks. We standardized overtime guidelines and eliminated jurisdictional barriers. Now there is no need to call maintenance to change a lightbulb. Many operations folk now do their own day-to-day maintenance. Now the reorganized, refocused buildings have more volume, and we produce the best laundry products in the marketplace.

Asked how this growing trust and openness in communication came about, McDonogh adds, "Jack Welch has a direct impact on us. He sets the vision and standards for performance. Every quarter when the earnings report comes out we have improved from the year before. He sometimes doesn't get the credit he deserves. He is an exceptional leader. Jack's personal involvement with our transformation is a big reason Norm Mitchell and his team have hung in there and worked closely with us to keep the vision alive."

## SUMMARY OF LESSONS FROM GENERAL ELECTRIC APPLIANCES

- If liberated and empowered, workers can be partners in change.
- Labor-management dialogue must radically change.
- Invest in the labor force as the key to the future.
- Encourage truth telling as the basis of trust building.

# Chapter 8

—∿—

# THE CHILDREN'S HOSPITAL OF PITTSBURGH CASE

If you go to Children's Hospital of Pittsburgh (CHP) to admit your sick child, you immediately sense that this is a very special place. Your car is valet-parked. You enter through sliding doors to the elevator area, where clearly displayed signs point you to where you need to go. If you look lost, friendly health care workers don't wait for you to ask for directions; they offer to help. You hear the laughter and the crying of children of all sizes and ethnic backgrounds and with various illnesses. You see the worried and the relieved looks on parents' and children's faces. When you go to admissions with your child, you experience an intense, noisy, businesslike, but friendly hour or more punctuated by the constant traffic to and from the à la cart food station in the area.

If, after leaving admissions, you are sent to 7 South, the Orthopedic Neurosurgical Unit, you experience a pleasing respite in stark contrast to the admissions area. This unit is the first to roll out the new patient care model developed as part of CHP's reengineering process. On entering 7 South, you are greeted first by art that is created by the children who are patients there. Then, as you turn the corner, you are greeted by a health unit coordinator, who welcomes you. Your child is assigned to a room decorated in subdued, yet inviting, colors and patterns. As a parent you can stay with the child for as long as you want. If you decide to stay overnight, you can settle into the foldout bed. You can order your own meal trays from the child's menu. You can watch TV or view videotapes or participate in parent education seminars. As your child is lovingly cared for, you become a part of the community of healing. The unit nurses and other professionals in this family-centered culture attend to the needs of parent and child.

Today, at the pinnacle of its success, Children's Hospital of Pittsburgh confronts what all U.S. health care institutions face: a climate of "managed care" in which the price of care delivery determines who gets to serve the patients. In this suddenly competitive climate, hospitals like CHP need to be competitive on prices at the same time that they continue to improve the quality of and access to care.

The challenges of these developments are many. For one thing, it means a complete redefinition of the way hospitals are run and the way health care providers relate to one another. It also means cutting costs dramatically in order to survive. To these ends, in 1994 CHP launched Vision 2001, a hospital-wide reengineering movement designed to reduce costs by $30 million over three years and to maintain and improve quality and efficiency simultaneously. This is how the Vision 2001 team described the changing environment and the new direction needed as managed care increased:

- Price of care delivery will be the primary driver of decision making by payors—quality and customer service will be [the payor's] secondary concern.
- To be price competitive, we will need to provide services in a less expensive manner.
- Patient access to care must be improved both in terms of site care delivery and also in the admissions and discharge processes.
- There will be greater emphasis on outpatient and home care.

- We must increase our efforts to be the voice of children to ensure that their needs are addressed in this managed care arena.
- Children's Hospital and its medical staff must work together as never before in order to adapt to this new environment.

Can Children's Hospital of Pittsburgh continue to provide unparalleled medical care to children and their families? Can it reposition itself in a competitive marketplace in a way that honors its health care professionals, who must now redefine their roles as they work smarter and more efficiently? These are questions that remain to be answered. In the meantime the hospital is taking bold steps to reorient itself to the future. As it does so, it evokes the inevitable symptoms of change for its employees: anxiety, stress, and ambivalence. This is a story that offers some important lessons about healing health care survivors and the "customers" they serve.

Caught in the midst of the health care revolution, Children's Hospital of Pittsburgh stands poised to be a model for change. This is nothing new for CHP. Over its long history, the hospital has earned the distinction of being one of the nation's leaders in providing comprehensive and specialized care for children. It houses the largest pediatric ear, nose, and throat department and the largest poison center in the U.S., as well as the largest diabetic clinic in North America. CHP has consistently made *U.S. News & World Report*'s annual list of the best pediatric hospitals in the U.S., recently being ranked fifth among the top twenty-three. The 235-bed facility serves a regional population of about five million and has admitted children from more than fifty foreign countries.

In January 1986 the city of Pittsburgh celebrated the opening of CHP's new multimillion dollar home. Two years later, the hospital expanded again with the opening of an outpatient satellite in Wexford, Pennsylvania. Then, in 1990 it unveiled yet another major success—the $15 million government-funded Rangos Research Center. This was around the same time that the hospital launched its Star Bright Centennial Campaign in recognition of its first one hundred years of operation. The celebration was designed to reemphasize the hospital's mission, the main elements of which are

- excellence in comprehensive care;
- education and research for the health of infants, children, and young adults;
- service that provides children and their families compassionate, state-of-the-art care in a cost-effective manner.

When the senior staff at CHP decided to embark on the reinvention of the hospital to survive economic challenges, they were driven by a primary concern: "Patient care quality and our role in education and research must not suffer as we change to reduce costs." Then as now they took pride in the roles they play in state-of-the-art research, in the education of health care professionals, and in the excellent support systems for parents and children that have been given consistently high ratings on customer surveys. In fact, their goal was to achieve better patient care and better support as they lowered costs.

The staff came together to brainstorm and plan in a series of interdisciplinary team meetings. The key questions that drove their early deliberations were What are the systems that drive our organization? How do they work? How well do they work? What is our model of patient care? The breakthrough answer to this last question, which by the way is a most important one to ask as an organization prepares to reengineer itself, came from a cardiologist. His view was that the hospital's care model was much like a planetary system in which "we orbit around each other, but don't connect." This insight provided the impetus to create a new, reengineered model of care for CHP.

The reengineering process at Children's Hospital of Pittsburgh could be a good case study for organizations in any sector seeking to reinvent themselves. Going into the process, the staff took great care to involve people at all levels. The goal was to get the best input possible. At the same time the leadership hoped to involve employees in decisions that affected them. Doing so would help to ensure that morale was not irreparably damaged as survivors changed the way they worked together under the new model for serving children and their families.

Grassroots multidisciplinary teams that represented a cross section of people from all levels became part of the Vision 2001 reengineering process. As described by Mary Kay Loughran, executive vice president of Patient Care Services,

> We believe that frontline people who know the patients are key to making the changes work. So we involved departments such as dietary, social work, environmental services, and administration, as well as nurses and physicians. We assigned them in mixed groups to come up with a new model of patient care in which all the pieces were integrated. They designed a model in which the child and family are at the center of our work as we offer a continuum of care that guarantees that, whether you are an inpatient or outpatient, the hospital knows your every need. This model facilitates communication and interactions that are aimed at the highest quality of clinical care.

Working with American Practice Management, CHP underwent an institution-wide redesign. The four-stage process was an intense, revolutionary approach in which the hospital literally set out to reinvent itself. The initiative was headed by a Steering Committee made up of board members, senior administrative staff, and physician leaders. The role of the Steering Committee included providing leadership throughout the process, establishing cost-saving targets, reviewing and approving or rejecting recommendations from all reengineering teams, ensuring that technology needs were not neglected, and planning, organizing, and monitoring implementation.

Like organizations everywhere, CHP went through the painful process of downsizing and restructuring needed to survive. By 1996 roughly 250 positions hospital-wide had been eliminated, primarily by attrition. The hospital had successfully cut its bureaucracy, reducing the layers of management from seven to four. It had cut over 20 percent of the management costs.

During this difficult de-layering transition, many senior staff members left. Reengineering typically requires that an organization wipe the slate clean and start over from scratch. This means that people get displaced in the process and literally have to reapply for jobs. Some employees went through the interview process and succeeded; others didn't. Some accepted early retirement packages. And some simply opted out of the hospital because they were uncomfortable with the ambiguity associated with the changes. Survivors reacted in the usual ways: anxiety, insecurity, lowered morale, and anger.

The healing began with new blood after the displacements. A new senior staff was installed, sending a clear message that things had changed. The major challenge after the upheaval was rebuilding trust. Survivors who could live with ambiguity and transformational change did well in this, according to Loughran.

As they moved forward, the CHP reengineering team set about the task of identifying roles and work processes to carry out the new model and reduce costs. As the patient model was rolled out, some services remained centralized and some were decentralized, all based on the input of the physician- and employee-led teams. A Patient Care Team oversaw improvements to the actual delivery of care. A Purchased Goods and Services Team looked at the kinds of medical and surgical supplies being used. Everything from catheters to disposable diapers to service contracts were reviewed in an attempt to identify cost-saving opportunities. Along with the clinical staff, the Administrative Support Team reassessed support services. The Clinical Resources Management Team examined clinical pathways and guidelines for care and reevaluated how such matters as X rays and pharmaceuticals were being handled. In short, every corner of the hospital was reengineered.

Since physicians generally are extremely busy and typically autonomous, achieving their support of this process was key.

There was a physician cochair on every design team, much to the credit of medical director J. R. Zuberbuhler. The physicians made time to support the process of change and give critical input.

Finally, the Human Resources Committee played a pivotal role. Its charge was to oversee the human dynamics of change in order to ensure that employees' needs were met during and after Vision 2001. The committee also worked jointly with the Communications Team to clearly convey human resources issues, policies, and programs to employees, physicians, and the general community.

## LESSONS FROM CHILDREN'S HOSPITAL OF PITTSBURGH

Recognizing that the majority of the present workforce would continue to need support in making the necessary changes and regaining emotional security concerning the new order, the agents of change at Children's Hospital of Pittsburgh have focused intensively on planning for survivors. Employees have been engaged and supported in several very successful ways as their journey toward healing continues. In the process they have taught us some important lessons about ways to revitalize the workforce after reengineering. Following are three key steps for survivors at CHP and the lessons learned in each case.

### *Training Is an Investment, Not an Expense*

The Training and Organization Development Team has been charged with ensuring that employees are supported and involved in every way possible. Their goal is to encourage all employees to support the development of Children's Hospital of Pittsburgh as a "learning organization" at the same time that they develop themselves professionally. The team adopted the following position and guiding principles, designed to "create an environment in which all can thrive":

During the reengineering process, the CHP environment will be characterized by a commitment to promote individual learning. This learning will result in practice changes in the way individuals and the organization operate, resulting in more efficient operations, more satisfied customers and higher levels of financial performance. . . . The following tenets will serve as the guiding principles: 1. Executive leadership, management and staff must recognize the need to learn and to pursue learning opportunities. 2. As a learning organization, Children's Hospital fosters education by providing formal and informal learning opportunities. 3. Change and learning are closely related: change is facilitated through the education of the people who must effect any change program. 4. Learning is an investment, not an expense.

CHP's commitment to education and learning includes teaching parents about childhood diseases, attracting and educating the best MDs in the country, and providing ongoing education for nurses, patient care partners, service assistants, and the hospital staff in general.

In the aftermath of reengineering, the biggest concern of the senior administration was how to maintain professional excellence and support the new skills required as redesigned work processes led people to do different jobs. For example, in the area of patient care, the nurse's job was impacted in a major way. Many routine tasks that nurses typically performed were now delegated to a new group of health care workers called patient care partners (PCPs). These jobs included feeding patients, holding and comforting crying children for long periods, bathing, transporting patients, and making beds. They were activities that the reengineering teams, which included nurses, decided did not require a registered nurse's license to be performed well. The goal was to focus RNs on the work of nursing, thereby improving patient care. By delegating specific duties to the PCPs, nurses would be freed up to focus more closely on the critical professional aspects of care, like assessing and monitoring patients, preventing complications, providing patient and family education, and evaluating the outcomes of the care delivered.

All of this has spelled major training and retraining for both nurses and PCPs. Nurses now have to learn skills like supervising and delegating to PCPs. With the constant unveiling of new health care technology, nursing education in this reengineered organization now spans technical, interpersonal, and supervisory skill building. Likewise, the patient care partners have to be reoriented and retrained. PCPs are typically certified medical workers who have attended community college to become medical assistants. They may be emergency medical technicians (EMTs) or respiratory technicians who have worked in health care. The PCPs must be retrained from the perspective of pediatric care delivery. They are hired by RNs and their manager using strict guidelines for screening. Preceptor nurses then supervise their on-the-job training. Eventually the PCPs are paired with RNs in a partnering relationship.

From the hospital's and reengineering team's perspective this is working smarter and improving care. From the perspective of the nurses forced to let go of what was familiar and what represented their professional identity, it is a difficult road to travel. The very nurses who for years complained about work overload now have to be assisted through the emotional trauma of letting go of parts of their jobs that were familiar, routine, and comfortable. Some nurses expressed fear that the addition of PCPs might threaten their jobs. They felt pressures as they struggled to make changes, integrate the PCPs into their work life, and keep up with their busy schedule. In a survey the nurses expressed their feelings about these changes this way:

> I love my job at CHP. Quality of clinical care and nursing care must not be compromised as we change to become more cost-conscious. Money is not the single motivational factor in running this place.

> Parents are concerned about the use of PCPs. I worry that they might lose faith in us with these changes.

I believe change is needed but change will bring a decrease in my level of satisfaction. As my time with each of my patients decreases, so will their confidence in me. Most of my patients trust and rely on me for many different reasons and I want to be able to continue to provide the support, education, and time for them. I don't see this as a possibility in the future as other support staff fill the gaps of time for my patients. The patient will get the care he needs from many people. What about my job satisfaction?

This last sentiment represents the pain of loss that many nurses experience and is one of the key areas of concern as the hospital figures out how to support survivors through the changes. As Mary Kay Loughran sees it,

Training and organizational development are key. Through these activities we minimize the losses employees feel in going through a difficult, sweeping change. More importantly, it will allow us to maintain and enhance our professional excellence. Through training, our employees not only learn different and better ways of doing things, they also learn to "think outside of the box" as they work in a new environment. Physicians and other caregivers need to be trained in the new organizational dynamics as we become more team oriented. They must also learn about the old versus the new health care realities in our rapidly changing economy and the implications for themselves as professional leaders whose roles are changing. But we must keep in mind one of the most important lessons learned: we must remind people what of the old works well and should be kept, and what is new and should be embraced as we go forward. We always remind people of two things: "Don't throw the baby out with the bathwater," and "Let's make it better for ourselves so we can make it better for families."

## Communication Is Everything

In the start-up phase of the reengineering process, the Communications Design Team played, as it continues to play, a pivotal role in administering to survivor wounds. Employees naturally worried about their future and expected the worst. Anticipating and responding to employees' concerns, the team adopted several communications strategies, including a newsletter, hot lines, town meetings, and an open-door policy on the part of the vice presidents and the CEO Paul Kramer. In the initial stages employees attended town meetings at which they were updated on the Steering Committee's activities and the accomplishments of the reengineering teams. Employees wrote questions on three-by-five-inch index cards and received responses at the town meetings. "Talking Points," a bulletin attached to the hospital's employee newsletter, answered the most commonly asked questions from the town meetings for the benefit of those unable to attend. After a year or so, attendance at the town meetings dwindled. The feedback received from employees about the various communications strategies was that the information was good but not received fast enough.

CHP then hired a new director of public relations, whose primary focus has been to streamline the process and get feedback and information across more quickly and effectively to the hospital staff and physicians. I first met this new director, Deann Marshall, at a leadership meeting at which team members reported on the status of their various reengineering initiatives. As the meeting unfolded, she was completing the latest fact sheet for employees. I later secured a copy of this important employee communiqué, titled "Vision 2001 Update." It included an overview of completed initiatives and gave a financial update: "To date, 93% ($27,779K) of the $30 million target has been approved by the Vision 2001 Steering Committee. The project is on pace to achieve the financial target of $15 million in savings in fiscal year 1996. Implementation plans and monitoring processes will be in place to closely track cost savings and quality over the next six months."

The update then turned to the matter most closely related to survivor anxiety: employee retention. The message in this section was that human resources training for managers was under way and that this training was designed to "retain qualified, successful employees." It went on to explain that each department would be assisted in identifying its human resource needs to ensure that "open positions will be first filled by qualified internal candidates."

In the question-and-answer section that followed, twenty-three employee queries were printed, along with honest answers in plain English. The first employee question was "What happens if my position on my unit is eliminated? What options do I have?" The second question was "Describe how the new Patient Care Model will affect staffing." The remaining questions addressed a variety of concerns, including such matters as how to secure training, how to apply for a PCP position, and whether retraining was paid for by the hospital.

The answers were frank and to the point, laying out the procedures that human resources and the employees' managers would use to assist survivors in being placed elsewhere ("every effort will be made to retain good, competent employees") or, if no comparable positions were available, to offer "other options," including severance pay. The new model, the "Vision 2001 Update" explained, would change the mix of full-time and part-time employees to achieve more staffing flexibility. It would "increase the number of part-time positions and decrease the number of full-time positions" and "create new positions, including the Patient Care Partners (PCPs), whose skills overlap those of the current RNs and Patient Care Assistants." Training would be required by all and paid for by the hospital. The communiqué then added the most important point from the patient's perspective: "The model will increase caregiver hours per patient, although the mix of providers will change."

As demonstrated above by the nurses' responses to retraining and redesigning their jobs, this information does little to minimize survivors' anxiety about preserving the past. But it is factual, honest, and timely information that ultimately goes a long way toward preserving the integrity of the hospital's leadership team. It demonstrates a commitment to come clean with the facts. And as the Westinghouse Nuclear Services Division's "Reality '95" course demonstrated, survivors armed with the truth ultimately can be fuller participants in making informed choices aimed at shaping their future. In her words the public relations director's commitment is "to communicating about the process with no sugarcoating of news." She works closely with the Vision 2001 team and with the employees affected. She communicates by walking around, as does the CEO and other members of the senior staff. Employees feel comfortable taking their feedback and questions to her office as well as communicating via E-mail, by phone calls, and in meetings.

While there are still large pockets of fear, including employees who would not identify their departments on the hospital's Organizational Effectiveness Survey and employees who complain to the media about their low morale level, it is clear that the reengineering team will continue its focus on employee involvement and intensified communications. The results from the survey will be shared with the entire hospital community, for example, followed by focus group discussions with a cross section of employees to get concrete feedback and suggestions to improve the process of change at CHP.

## *The First Commitment Must Be to Quality of Care*

Everyone I spoke to at Children's Hospital of Pittsburgh about "quality customer service" corrected my lingo. The first time this occurred was in a meeting with physicians as I discussed plans for rolling out their Organizational Effectiveness Survey. I mentioned the importance of feedback from employees in ensuring quality customer service. A physician said, "I beg your pardon, but we do not call our patients customers around here. We are caregivers, working with patients and their families."

Later, when I interviewed the executive vice president, a former nurse, she explained to me that "We never refer to patients as customers because we are a hospital, not a factory. We deliver care. This thinking is behind all our efforts, even our decision to offer valet parking when families found it too difficult to find parking in this area."

Hospitals deal with human lives, so mistakes in a reengineering health care environment can be fatal. Under the watchful eyes of patients, the media, and employees themselves any move that jeopardizes safety or the quality of care will become a rallying event against the changes. Caregivers who are charged with making the transformation work at CHP endure the usual stresses associated with downsizing and restructuring. Like survivors in every sector discussed so far, they must learn to work differently, and they must make the time to improve their skills and competencies as their job content, roles, and relationships change. In addition, the health caregiver has the added burden of being viewed under a microscope for the first bit of evidence that care is being compromised. The lesson for the engineering team is clear. As the hospital moves into the final phases of the process, it must find ways to provide the support systems that the staff needs to continue to perform maximally.

Children's Hospital of Pittsburgh has a strong academic mission to supply well-trained and educated pediatric professionals and is nationally regarded as one of the best teaching hospitals. As mentioned earlier, the hospital is also among the top echelons in patient care. As reengineering takes place, there is a lot of pressure not to compromise this excellent standing in any way. This is the reason the Vision 2001 team involved a cross section of employees in leading the changes. In retrospect, it is felt that even more patient care people could have been included on the teams so as to ensure the best input concerning quality. An important learning in this process has been, according to Mary Kay Loughran, that "People can help cut costs and improve quality if you simply ask them how, instead of going to the sweeping layoffs some companies are using these days."

## SUMMARY OF LESSONS FROM CHILDREN'S HOSPITAL OF PITTSBURGH

- Training is an investment, not an expense.
- Communication is everything; get and give continual input.
- The first commitment must be to quality of care.

*Part III*

—◆—

# CHARTING
# THE FUTURE

## Chapter 9

—m—

# ATTENDING TO OTHER
# SIDE EFFECTS

To promote organizational healing we must change our work
habits and managerial behavior in the variety of ways that have
been illustrated throughout this book. We must also attend to
several complications associated with the trauma of transforming organizations. Among these are

- the impact of low morale;
- the ethical quandaries of downsizing;
- the challenge of valuing diversity in a downsizing organization;
- the dilemmas of managing in the dark;
- the split between labor and management.

Each of these complications can derail the organization's attempt to revolutionize itself for the future. Yet, if managed
well, each holds significant opportunities for promoting a
healthier organization. In this chapter I will examine these five
complications and then offer treatment options. In chapter 10
I will present prescriptions for letting go of the old covenant
and for renegotiating a new social contract.

# THE IMPACT OF LOW MORALE

Healthy workplaces, where employees bring all of themselves to work, feel valued and valuable, find job satisfaction, and are hopeful about the future, are a rarity. Most organizations these days suffer from a serious sickness of spirit. "Nonessential" workers furloughed during the 1995 and 1996 U.S. government shutdowns returned to work angry and demoralized by the experience. They speak in my leadership seminars of their sense of worthlessness and expendability and suggest that their commitment is waning. Women and minorities continue to wrestle with subtle and not so subtle forms of discrimination, while white men claim that they are becoming the "new minorities."

Business managers, eyeing the de-layering of colleagues in their ranks, nervously wonder about their own expendability. Some joke, with a tinge of seriousness, that the next wave of unionism may well come from the ranks of management and salaried workers who feel insecure about their corporate future. We wonder if this may not be possible as the United Steelworkers of America diversifies its membership to include lawyers, nurses, bus drivers, and county and municipal workers in some parts of the country.

Health care professionals and managers tensely await the final impacts of managed care as their roles rapidly change and their anxiety about the future escalates. Educators debate newfangled ideas like school choice and charter schools as they nervously watch what was familiar and secure evolve into something unfamiliar and uncertain. No sector and few organizations are exempt from the pangs of change in our downsizing, restructuring economy.

Even in seemingly robust companies employees and managers speak matter-of-factly about "low morale," as though it came hand in hand with being at work. In the same breath they talk about "too much change." No doubt change and low morale go hand in hand. Change breeds apprehension, because every change is an affront to our competence, our comfort zone, our certainty about the future, and our well-protected identity. Excessive change or sweeping transformational change that calls for a rethinking of everything we have taken for granted can have devastating effects on the esprit de corps of the workforce.

This is not to say that these changes aren't necessary in the present economic situation. It is simply a reminder that, to heal downsizing, restructuring organizations, we must acknowledge and resolve the human emotional side effects of change, at the same time that we address the strategic business and technological challenges. Yet, this organizational healing process can be complicated and demanding.

Few managers have the time or the training to resolve the symptoms of shock, denial, anger, depression, distrust, and disorientation that are experienced by those who survive the layoffs and the turmoil as we reinvent organizations. As a result the side effect for mismanaged survivors and burned-out managers alike is low morale. As suggested earlier, low employee morale is the most readily discernable symptom that signals the dis-ease in organizations.

The major leadership challenge in the aftermath of downsizing is to re-create the work climate and culture so that survivors can rebuild their self-esteem, find work satisfying, and become motivated to achieve at or beyond the levels they did prior to restructuring. Everywhere, managers I consult with pose the question, How do we improve morale and motivate employees to embrace the changes? I remind them that they cannot treat low morale. It is a symptom, not a cause. The best they can hope to do is to create a motivating environment. To do so requires an understanding of how human motivation works and how it is related to individual and organizational needs.

I believe that most people enter the workplace turned on and hopeful. Their workplace experience may quickly turn them off and dash their hopes. Workers also arrive with personal needs and motives that determine why they sought or accepted a given job, whether they stay or leave voluntarily, and how they react when their future is threatened as others around them are forced to leave. If employees encounter a healthy, motivating environment, they continue to enjoy the work experience and to strive toward excellence. A motivating environment is one that encourages, inspires, or enables people to satisfy their needs. If motivated this way, workers apply their talents, experience, and interpersonal influence to achieve goals based on internal or external standards for performance. In a motivating environment morale tends to be high.

Organizational healing, in the context of this book, comes about when the workplace creates conditions that enable people to satisfy their basic needs so that they can create the outcomes they want. When an organization is in the process of transforming itself through downsizing, restructuring, reengineering, or other means, people's (and the organization's) comfort zone is disrupted by a series of unmet needs spawned by the changes. Unmet needs demotivate. Psychologist Abraham Maslow and others have taught us that, in order to be motivated and effective in the world, people must meet their physiological, then safety, and then social needs and then their need for esteem and, finally, their need to "self-actualize," or be their best. Similarly, David McClelland and other motivation theorists have identified three needs that motivate people in work situations. These are

- the need for achievement;
- the need for power;
- the need for affiliation.

In an organization that has recently restructured, or in which people have been laid off, these basic motivators are jeopardized for those who remain. Survivors typically doubt that they or the organization will continue to achieve at previous levels, and the work itself becomes less satisfying as they feel pressured to do more with less. They feel victimized and powerless. They lose their vitality to feelings of low morale.

If managers and leaders are not guided by the behavior exemplified by healthy organizations, the situation is compounded further. In addition to the loss of motivators, "dissatisfiers" also come into play in the downsized organization. These are factors that, if not managed well, lead to dissatisfaction. According to Frederick Herzberg, a leading researcher on motivation, potential dissatisfiers are remarkably consistent with the conditions that erode employee morale:

- poor supervisory practices;
- "unfriendly" company policy;
- ineffective relationships with peers, supervisors, and subordinates;
- disrupted personal life;
- challenging working conditions;
- poor incentives to perform or inadequate salary and benefits;
- extreme job insecurity or extreme job security.

It is important to understand that the factors (motivators) leading to job satisfaction, excellence, and productivity are distinct from those leading to job dissatisfaction. Removing dissatisfiers does *not* make work more satisfying; adding motivators does. When dissatisfiers are removed, workers move to a neutral place. By enriching the work and introducing motivators—opportunities for achievement, power, and affiliation—managers can then restore employee morale as they support and inspire workers to be and do their best. In short, improved morale comes after the employee and employer negotiate a new social and psychological contract rooted in mutual concern and trust. The details of such a contract will be explored in chapter 10.

# THE ETHICAL QUANDARIES OF DOWNSIZING

In November 1995 I was invited to speak at the Pittsburgh Theological Seminary in response to the comments of PPG Industries' CEO J. E. Dempsey. The topic of the seminary's forum was "The Practical and Ethical Costs of Corporate Reengineering." Dempsey spoke eloquently and sincerely about the old versus the new corporate social contract. He shed much light on the "sweeping forces" that are driving changes in his industry today: global competition, deregulation, and technological advances. No one could disagree with his depiction of our current reality. I agreed with everything he was saying. Audience members nodded in agreement as he spoke about moving "from paternalism to partnering." He then added a fourth driving force: shareholder expectations.

The ethics of allowing shareholder demands to motivate downsizing decisions became the rallying point of protest from many audience members. Following our presentation, they asked loaded questions like Don't you think that it's unethical for shareholder greed to drive the decision to downsize? and Don't you think corporations have a responsibility to the community of workers that goes beyond just making more profits?

After our panel discussion was over, people milled around, the question of the ethics of downsizing and restructuring still fully present. One woman pulled me aside and told me that, while she was most impressed by everything I had to say about the dilemmas of managing and leading in this new environment and about the responsibility of workers to seek training and exercise more personal control over their livelihood and their work, she could not get past the idea that companies have a responsibility to society to provide job security.

The session aggravated my growing ambivalence about this subject. It is easy to understand the business reasons for downsizing and restructuring. I believe strongly that employees must share in the responsibility for creating more satisfying relationships with their employers and that our economic health and well-being may depend on an ability to let go of the old contract, which, by the way, is a stereotype, and create a more practical contract for the future. But where does the employer's responsibility end and the employee's begin? How do we resolve the ethical dilemmas inherent in this situation?

When an organization hires an employee, it clearly expects the employee to invest himself or herself in company-specific skills. The employee must be fully present, investing his or her time in learning about the organization, adapting to its ways of doing work, and securing the training and skills necessary to enable the entity to succeed. In so doing the employee assumes the risk that the skills learned within the confines of the organization may not be transferable to other organizations. So, in a sense, employee loyalty and devotion are still expected to some degree. Yet, in most organizations this can no longer be reciprocated with a promise of security.

The question of ethics in our downsizing culture is the topic of discussion from conference rooms to plant floors, from interoffice memos to the Internet. World Wide Web news groups and on-line forums now find dislocated employees and survivors, managers, and academics "chatting" about the "grim reaper of downsizing" and depicting this new strategy as "the drive-by shootings of corporate America." They ask for and offer advice on how to cope. Among these electronically transmitted opinions and musings, I came across a reference to an article published by Denis Collins, professor of business ethics at the University of Wisconsin-Madison, in the *Wisconsin State Journal* on December 31, 1995. His open letter to business offered a novel prescription aimed at stemming the hemorrhaging of the American workplace:

> Despite the current trend in downsizing, and the ecstasy of Wall Street every time a company announces a major layoff, the most socially responsible action a company engages in is employing people. . . . Meanwhile, you have downsized and reengineered your organization until it can no longer be any leaner or meaner. But the employees who have survived don't

seem to be as cheery as they should be during this holiday season.

'Tis the season to make a new year's resolution for your organization. Pledge that you will re-employ everyone you laid off at challenging jobs that will expand your company's business. Having eliminated all of your organization's redundancies, it is now time for you to think of expansion. The survivors miss these people and feel somewhat guilty, rather than proud, of their survival status.

Put the survivors in small groups and have them brainstorm ways in which the company could expand that would result in the re-employment of those recently laid off. Are there new markets to explore? Are their niche opportunities in old markets? How could your company productively and profitably use the services of these former employees? Watch how quickly their depression turns into creativity and joy. . . . Recently laid-off management and nonmanagement employees with twenty to thirty years of organizational experience are wondering about the meaning of life. So are the survivors. Give them all a helping hand and put some fun back into work again.

In attempting to resolve the ethical dilemma of cutting employees to ensure profits, some argue that shareholders assume the greatest risks and therefore earn the right to require drastic measures to assure an adequate return on their investment. Others argue that employees assume an equal risk by investing themselves, their commitment, and their talents in the organization. Consequently, they should have equal voice in the leadership of their organizations. Pointing to examples of whole towns laid waste by plant closings, the erosion of a community's tax base, and other devastating side effects of layoffs, some take the position that all organizations exist as part of the larger community and as such have a social responsibility to provide ongoing employment, even if it results in lower profits. While many corporate leaders are aware of and concerned about this impact, most argue that in the end attempts to preserve jobs and communities fly in the face of the economic realities of a rapidly changing world. They remind us that the survival of the business and our long-term economic viability are at stake.

Situational ethicists would likely conclude that the solution lies in a combination of all of the above. Organizations ultimately must address these ethical dilemmas by finding ways to negotiate creatively so that needs of shareholders, customers, employees, employers, and the larger community are all taken into account in the healing process. For example, employers demonstrate good faith when they make every effort to explore and use alternatives like hiring freezes, reduced work hours, and early retirements to cut costs in ways that ultimately save jobs and send the message that employees are valued resources, even in hard times.

## THE CHALLENGE OF VALUING DIVERSITY

A central theme in downsizing organizations is how to use limited resources more creatively. This is compounded by the fact that to create an organization that survives in the emerging global marketplace managers must create and sustain work teams that can integrate and apply diverse perspectives across differences in gender, ethnicity, race, values, personalities, and abilities. Cross-functional teams, total quality management, self-directed teams, employee involvement—all of the organizational trends aimed at improving quality and productivity and cutting costs in downsizing, restructuring organizations imply an ability to value and manage diversity. For all of these important strategies to work in a leaner, meaner multinational marketplace, we must create truly inclusive organizations whose cultures support development of everyone's talents and skills.

Yet, paradoxically, workforce diversity poses a major challenge to healing the downsized organization. This is the brewing controversy that survivors whisper about but few are brave enough to articulate in the conference rooms of America. Organizations committed to creating a multicultural mix of workers struggle with the dilemmas posed when layoffs are necessary. Women and minorities who are survivors face the same symptoms of survivor sickness outlined in this book. And they face the added concerns that, being the "last hired," they will be the "first fired." Women, racial and ethnic minorities, immigrants, people with disabilities, and those different from the organization man in other ways also argue that they were never really part of the old covenant.

"We've never known job security," an African American woman in one of my diversity sessions pointed out when the inevitable subject of downsizing came up. "In a way it makes me scared that we are cutting jobs. Yet in another way this insecurity is nothing new for me."

A white woman in the same group responded, "I can relate to what you're saying. Twenty years ago I hid the fact that I was married because secretaries were expected to leave once they got married, and especially if they got pregnant."

There is a growing concern among minorities that downsizing will further exacerbate their history of job discrimination. In organizations in which downsizing focuses on seniority—leaning toward early retirement options—the complication of last hired, first fired is not a major threat to women and minorities, who are the newest workforce entrants. And as we are learning from studies about survivor syndrome, survivors' fears do not need statistical validation to be real.

The following comment from a white man in response to women's comments in the same diversity session provides a typical example: "We are insecure too. It's not just downsizing that's posing a threat. Everyday I see women and minorities taking our jobs!"

Another white man added, "According to the statistics I'm hearing, we are becoming the new minority."

To this an African American man in the group responded, "It makes me angry when white men in this class say, 'We're becoming the new minority.' In my opinion you're upset because with all the downsizing going on you are experiencing the insecurity that minorities have always felt."

A member of the company's bargaining unit summed up the exchange this way: "It's all about who has power and who doesn't. Those of us who are nonexempt have the same discussions in union meetings when we talk about our relationship with management."

When employees in a session such as the one illustrated above step back from their positions and explore the assumptions behind each comment, they slowly come to realize that all group members share the same feelings: anger, ambivalence, insecurity, fear, and lack of trust. And they typically comment on how difficult it is for them to become allies for one another in a workplace where everyone is feeling insecure. Yet, being allies for one another is what most trainers preach in courses on valuing and managing diversity. Very little is said about the healing that must first occur if such relationships are to be built in a downsized organization.

Unless we are committed to healing the wounds of gender bias, racial and ethnic discrimination, and labor-management differences, the wounds of downsizing only deepen. Some organizations are making strides in this area. It is interesting to note that the impetus for change often comes from employees themselves. But unless senior management is committed to creating a more inclusive organization, the healing process cannot begin.

John Sartin, manager of Global Sourcing and Productivity Programs for General Electric, provides a good example of how this process is working at his company. "We believe in stretching people and helping them be their best. This means that we must challenge the company to create an inclusive, supportive culture in which everyone can perform to their highest capacity." Women and minorities who aspired to be equal players at the decision-making table, helping to shape their company's future, and who wanted to develop their talents and fulfill their career aspirations were disappointed that this was not always possible for them. So they took their concerns to CEO Jack Welch.

As an African American man, Sartin speaks with satisfaction of Welch's willingness to respond to the challenge of diversity. The CEO's response was to ask what the company should be doing differently. In so doing, he empowered minorities and women to take steps to improve GE's management of diversity as the company repositioned itself for the future. Sartin says, "In four years we have seen important gains in access to mentoring and promotions. We went from zero women in executive positions to thirteen. We now have a CEO and two vice presidents who are African American. Welch's buy-in was key to creating these changes."

The strides in the executive and managerial ranks at companies like GE, while encouraging, do not begin to address the larger condition that plagues the American labor force and that further complicates issues of diversity: the growing shortage of skilled workers. The reengineered organization will survive only if it attracts and develops workers with the right mix of human, conceptual, and technical skills. It is not just the computer expert that will survive in the new workplace, as many are led to believe. It is the worker who is service oriented toward the customer, who is comfortable working on self-directed work teams, and who has the interpersonal and problem-solving skills to achieve competitive outcomes on such teams. It is the worker who is comfortable with cross-training for more general assignments and who embraces and vigorously pursues lifelong learning and constant retraining for himself or herself. And it is the worker who is technically skilled and computer literate.

The widening skills gap between the socioeconomic underclass of all races and backgrounds, who comprise the numerical majority of the workforce, and those of the so-called majority has resulted in what some now refer to as "an information underclass." A 1989 report of the U.S. Bureau of the Census indicated, for example, that 51 percent of African

Americans and about 60 percent of people of Hispanic descent had never used computers, compared to 40 percent of whites and 30 percent of Asians. Efforts to promote organizational wellness will be seriously hampered if this skills gap is not minimized, since having the right skills mix determines who enters the workplace in the first place, who leaves, and who is able to survive in a downsizing economy. And this is not just an issue for the underclass. There is a shortage of available skilled workers, period.

Smart corporations realize that they must share the responsibility for upgrading the skills of the workforce for everyone, not just for those who have been traditionally excluded. The age of information and technology requires new and constantly renewed workforce skills. In this vein partnerships between business and education to ensure school-to-work transition are beginning to blossom.

So, at the same time that workforce diversity poses challenges it also presents an unprecedented opportunity for organizations to upgrade and tap the talents and perspectives of their diverse workers in order to meet the needs of an equally diverse body of customers. Organizations that are struggling to create renewed, effective entities out of chaos cannot ignore the need to build relationships across differences and to deal honestly with issues of power and loss of power. This makes good business sense. It is also the right thing to do. Consider the following business reasons for healing organizations through increased attention to diversity.

### *Improved Customer Service Through Employee Involvement*

If diverse members of a work team are fully included and better educated in ways of working together, this fosters open, accurate feedback and the full sharing of the information that is needed to assure continuous improvement of service delivery. It also facilitates healthy conflict resolution across differences when dealing with both colleagues and customers.

## Improved Job Safety

Occupations like law enforcement and construction experience an important safety benefit when, through efforts at education in valuing and managing diversity, employees reduce their discomfort in partnering with someone whose difference previously made them uncomfortable. By developing greater trust and cooperation across differences in gender, sexual orientation, race, and so forth, employees are more comfortable communicating with and supporting one another, especially in emergency or hazardous situations.

## Enhanced Productivity and Creativity

Productivity and creativity are two areas in which the greatest losses are experienced following downsizing and restructuring. Learning to be more inclusive and to value differences in perspectives and ideas creates a climate that is healthier for several reasons. First, those who typically feel excluded can redirect their energies toward the work at hand rather than toward their frustrations about not fitting in. Second, in a climate in which all ideas are accessible, the organization benefits from the creativity that comes with diverse ideas. Third, most organizations want to be more competitive by broadening the mix of customers they serve. To the extent that the makeup of the workforce mirrors the mix of customers, the organization benefits from having a richer array of perspectives available in the decision-making process.

## More Effective Human Resources Management

Inclusive organizations are seen as the "place of choice" both for the best job candidates and for those already in the workplace. In addition, an organization that takes diversity into account as it reinvents itself creates a climate in which the management of performance is based on assuring that everyone has a voice in getting his or her needs met and in shaping the organization's success. It means that the management process will likely be two-way communication, in which straight feedback about performance strengths and weaknesses are frankly discussed and managed because people are not walking on eggshells, which is typical in organizations in which "differences" equal "discomfort." Much healing occurs in relation to human resources management when mentoring, coaching, and ultimately employee motivation and morale are not blocked by a failure to be fair and inclusive.

## THE DILEMMAS OF MANAGING IN THE DARK

The manager's job today is being redefined by an evolving economy in ways that are not yet fully discernable. As agents of change, managers are required to implement and supervise necessary changes in people, processes, tasks, organizational structure, and technology. Yet, there are few proven road maps since we have never gone down this path before. In chapter 3 I identified several dilemmas that compound the problem, among them the paradoxes of cutting jobs and building trust simultaneously, having to do more with fewer resources, and inviting risk taking and creativity in a climate in which the stakes are high.

There are many other paradoxes that challenge those who work and manage in our downsizing and restructuring climate. Survivor managers live with the conflict of wanting to attract and retain talented, committed, productive workers, while being painfully aware that job security is not a promise they can always keep. Managers and nonmanagers alike are ambivalent about the layoffs. They understand why the changes are necessary, but they are uneasy about dealing with the consequences. Double standards abound at all levels. For example, the same corporate employees who disdain stockholder mandates that may cost them their jobs are the first to refer to "nonessential" government workers as "excesses—blatant examples of how badly our tax dollars are being spent."

"We probably shouldn't have hired them in the first place" is the usual response when the same employees who are outraged at corporate cutbacks are the stakeholders whose tax dollars are involved.

Phrases like "thinking outside of the box" and "upside-down thinking" have become popular in the jargon of reinventing organizations. These new ways of thinking are offered as antidotes for managing our way through the chaos of revolutionary change. In a sense managing in the dark requires that managers learn to go with the flow in an environment in which everything is turned upside down anyway. In a positive sense, managing these side effects of change by allowing ourselves to challenge some of the ways we have traditionally thought about work and the workplace allows us to release latent creative energy in our organizations.

As suggested throughout this book, healing a downsized organization means that managers must redefine how they do what they do and how they view those they supervise. They must move from scorekeeper to coach and leader. They must move from giving orders to delegating responsibility and collaborating with employees. They must re-create the workplace so that it welcomes, rather than fears, change. They must move from a posture of command and control to one of empowerment. They must shift from incidental on-the-job training to providing lifelong education for everyone. They must defy the boundaries of departmental structures and create interdisciplinary process teams. They must find creative ways to balance shareholder wishes with employee and customer needs. They must shift from compensating job activities to compensation based on profits and results for the customer. In short, the manager must energetically find ways to create exciting new beginnings out of paradox and chaos.

## THE LABOR-MANAGEMENT RIFT

As demonstrated in the story of General Electric Appliances in chapter 7, partnerships and joint labor-management problem solving and decision making are keys to healing organizational wounds. There is a tremendous amount of insecurity throughout the workplace on the part of those who are left behind. These days, this includes hourly and salaried workers and managers and nonmanagers alike.

In the words of labor leader Frank Mont, director of the Civil Rights Department of the United Steelworkers of America and director of the union's Dislocated Workers Programs,

> All employees—bargaining unit and nonbargaining unit—now feel less loyalty. But at the same time there is a growing awareness on the part of both management and labor that we have to come together and salvage the organization. We have a saying in our union: The management of a company is so important it can't just be left to managers anymore. And management must now realize that, when they hire workers, they don't check their brain at the door; they are not just "hands," [but] they are the brains behind the organization. Now labor and management must realize that the real threat is external and that they have to come together and work smarter internally. As workers, we invest our lives, not just our physical strength, to our businesses. We workers have taken the rap for producing shabby goods, but it has not been our fault. We in the union have consistently raised the question of quality and were told it's not our business. Now management is saying to us, What suggestions do you have for improving quality?

Mont has been a union member for forty-three years and manager for twenty-nine years. His perspective on labor-management issues has been sought by think tanks and boards over the years. When I posed the question of the role of unions in healing our downsizing economy, he told his story fully and passionately:

> Labor unions have played an important role in making sure severance packages for laid-off bargaining unit people are handled fairly. We have had the problem of layoffs and cyclical business challenges for a long time, so as union members we have become skilled at negotiating benefits to protect people.

While this was always an issue for the bargaining unit, it was never an issue for nonbargaining unit employees. Some management leaders were fair in dealing with bargaining unit employees during downsizing and restructuring. They got involved with the unions because they wanted to have a smooth transition for employees, including training [and] retraining. Some even provided corporate funds. Others were callous—they let the marketplace take care of it. The way they viewed us was "You are blue-collar workers. That's your lot in life."

Now that displacement has hit the ranks, it's a rude awakening for managers and other nonbargaining unit employees. A more enlightened management is emerging as the phenomenon of downsizing enters the white-collar ranks—a softening of attitudes. Recently Bethlehem Steel came forth with a lot of private dollars to help the downsizing transition as seventeen hundred people were being let go. They had meetings with union and management and involved everyone. They established dislocated worker centers funded with federal dollars, [the] Department of Labor, and the state of Pennsylvania's department of labor and industry, instituted training, and brought private companies on board to assist. This is important because the way that the displaced workers and their families are treated has an impact on how the surviving employees react and perform for the company.

But to truly heal, we have to work together to break down the differences even further. And we have to keep our word and be honest for trust to really develop. I'm not a cynic. But I've seen management revert back to old behaviors after workers have rallied around and helped them pull the company through. The hope I have is that the budding new relationships between union and management will be lasting ones. Our survival depends on it.

Employers must realize that they are community citizens. What they do affects the tax base in their community, their customers, employees, their families, the schools, the churches, and other business. They must come to grips with the fact that this is not just about shareholders' needs. In the long run social responsibility positions the corporations to perform better for stockholders and the employers.

## Chapter 10

—m—

# CHARTING A
# NEW EMPLOYEE/EMPLOYER
# CONTRACT

The procedure for promoting wellness in the downsized organization is twofold: get people to accept the new realities, and help them find ways to compensate for their tangible and psychological losses. Once this is accomplished, it becomes possible to focus everyone's attention on restoring all parts of the organizational body to a healthy state. If this is not achieved, or if it is done poorly, the organization and its members can be permanently scarred and disoriented by a lack of motivation, commitment, and stamina. The goal in healing the downsizing organization is to revitalize the members of the workforce so that they can become the kinds of partners in change which the organization needs for its survival. Today, the major barrier to achieving this goal is the absence of a social contract that works for both entities in the emerging economy. Behind this barrier lies a major opportunity: faced with the collapse of the old order, employee and employer can jointly chart a new understanding that satisfies the needs of both parties.

## RECOVERING FROM LESSONS OF THE PAST

Before charting a new contract, it is important to review our past history and understand how it shaped the old contract under which we labored. In the twenties, two-thirds of U.S. workers were in farming. By the sixties, two-thirds of workers were in manufacturing. Manufacturing efficiency became the model for other sectors, including banking, health care, government, and education. We came to believe in education that prepared workers to understand facts and follow orders. We lined children up in neat rows in the classroom and taught standardized lessons from standardized texts, preparing them for mass production.

From our earliest moments we were taught, "Go to school, get a diploma, and you will get a job." We were taught that the more education we attained, the greater our levels of success and security would be. We were sold on the idea that solid employment meant working in a single organization, and our pension plans, medical care, and other benefits were predicated on this myth of lifetime employment in a single company. Movement up the ladder of success was based on accomplishments over time as we progressed in our organization.

And, we were successful. Over time we evolved a strong industrial culture—a way of life, a set of deeply held beliefs—that informed our approach to making a living. We came to view our work as predictable, our employers as paternalistic, and our jobs as secure.

Today, as the industrial age evolves into the information age, two-thirds of U.S. workers are in the service sector. During the eighties, 46 percent of the Fortune 500 companies vanished from the list. Governments began slashing budgets and cutting employees and social programs. Manufacturing plants began closing or downsizing in record numbers. The utilities industry, perhaps the last bastion of stability and organized labor clout, began to be transformed by deregulation and competition. This industry is now also downsizing, restructuring, and changing the way it defines itself. Across all organizations employee benefits are now being cut and costs are being curtailed, along with funds for research and development and, in some sectors, for new ventures. At the same time mergers, acquisitions, and new alliances are being forged as organizations restructure, reinvent, and reengineer themselves and introduce new technology at a breathtaking pace.

The nature of the employee/employer relationship, born in the industrial age, is being reshaped by the realities of the nineties as organizations downsize and restructure for the future. Our deeply held cultural assumptions about work are being challenged, but we are seriously underprepared for the necessary transition. We were not taught that our skills may become obsolete, that our jobs might disappear, or that we might have to spend a lifetime reeducating ourselves to keep pace with changes in technology, markets, values, and the other forces driving change. We never expected that people would be laid off in droves and that even competent workers who successfully negotiated the hurdles of the corporate ladder could be gone tomorrow. Creating a support system outside the organization, being willing to take personal risks internally, being creative about our life choices, and demonstrating courage through personal leadership were neither taught nor rewarded.

## TOWARD A NEW EMPLOYEE/EMPLOYER CONTRACT

These changes signal the terms of the new contract. The emerging vocabulary of this contract is heard in business meetings and educational seminars. As discussed earlier, employers and a growing number of employees now speak of "thinking outside the box" and moving "from paternalism to partnering."

We are now in the midst of an organizational revolution in which employers are encouraging workers to demonstrate "ownership" and to "share leadership" on quality improvement teams and on reengineering committees. Employers are offering rewards tied to team outcomes and individual knowledge rather than to job activities. And, at the same time, employers are no longer guaranteeing security, except to the extent that employees can generate better customer satisfaction and profitability. To achieve these goals, a growing number of downsized organizations are outsourcing and subcontracting work to whoever will give them faster, cheaper, smarter service. This is a wake-up call for survivors. They cannot afford to miss the writing on the wall. The challenge is how to become as attractive as the outsourcing subcontractors to whom organizations now turn—how to become "the vendor of choice."

Upskilling the workforce is emerging as a key strategy. Experts in transforming organizations and managers are exploring the concept of lifelong learning as a path to ensuring a competitive workforce. At the same time policymakers, business leaders, and educators show growing concern about the absence of a skilled, flexible workforce suited to the demands of the emerging global economy. A 1990 report by the Committee for Economic Development, "Report on Demographics & Jobs," sums it up well: "We must close the troubling gap between the higher skill levels required in the new job market and the actual skills possessed by today's workers and labor force entrants [by establishing] a life cycle learning process transcending age boundaries, and [empowering] workers to adjust to changing circumstances."

Employers want workers who are positively oriented to change and who are willing to acquire the skills and competencies necessary to function effectively in a global, technology-driven, competitive marketplace. As discussed earlier, these needs are driven by regulatory demands, shareholder expectations, and other forces that combine to require greater efficiency, better customer service, and lower costs. To compete, organizations seek employees who are capable of helping meet these goals but who do not expect a job for life.

For their part employees seek "family-friendly companies" that are sensitive to shifting societal needs and values, as dual-career families and single parents search for ways to blend and balance important aspects of their lives. Employees want clarification on the opportunities and resources employers will, and will not, provide to assist them in managing their personal transitions. They want assurances that, while job security may no longer be a realistic expectation, they are still valued by and valuable to the organization. In this vein employers and employees are now beginning to espouse the personal and business benefits of valuing workforce diversity and of providing training and education that will better position employees both in their present workplaces and in the broader marketplace, should they have to move on.

Thus, as organizations make new demands of the workforce, workers must proactively see to their needs as well. The healthiest organizations are those in which this becomes a joint dialogue and a process of what Roger Fisher and William Ury refer to as "principled negotiation": In principled negotiation the parties are, simultaneously, "soft" on the relationship and "hard" on the problem. This means that they show concern for the task of getting the organization moving in the right direction and equal concern for the people involved. In their book *Getting to Yes* the authors explain it this way:

> It suggests that you look for mutual gains whenever possible, and that where your interests conflict, you should insist that the result be based on some fair standards independent of the will of either side. The method of principled negotiation is hard on the merits, soft on the people. It employs no tricks and no posturing. Principled negotiation shows you how to obtain what you are entitled to and still be decent.

To forge a new social contract, both employer and employee must let go of premises that are so deeply ingrained in our work culture that they remain out of our conscious awareness. These must be brought to the surface, examined, and redefined as employers and employees unlearn the expectations of the industrial age and reinvent their workplaces to adapt to the emerging economy. As we are successful, we will come to trust each other by developing healthier relationships based on interdependence.

There are pockets of change that are beginning to give us benchmarks for figuring out what the content of the new pact for the nineties and beyond might be. Arizona Public Service (APS) offers an example of a written social contract that the utility has incorporated into its 1995 strategic plan. Working with survivors in brainstorming sessions, the APS management literally negotiated the terms of the written contract. Employees took to the table demands such as more time for family, cross-training, and professional development and asked for assurances that there would be no repercussions if they took risks and failed. They also asked for clarification of the meaning of corporate buzzwords like "value-added."

APS management likewise took their own terms to the renegotiating process. They wanted employees to be flexible, to buy in to the necessary changes, and to be held personally accountable for their performances. Together they agreed on the following pact, titled "Our Company/Employee Understanding":

> We demonstrate commitment to our Company vision, mission and core values. We understand our jobs are not guaranteed — our employment is dependent on adding value to the organization and the success of our company. We are personally accountable for continuously finding ways to add value.

> We are committed to a work environment and culture that encourages us to make choices to achieve harmony and fulfillment in our work and personal lives. We are rewarded fairly, work in a safe and healthy environment, and pursue personal and professional development opportunities.

> Together, we are the future of the Company.

On the personal level, preparing ourselves to embrace employee/employer contracts like the one above will require tremendous positive energy and courageous leaps of faith as we let go of the myth of job security and seek new ways to assert and enhance our worth to the organization. But freeing ourselves to craft a new contract allows us to claim a degree of self-sufficiency that frees us from worrying about the next cuts. Granted that this is hard to do while facing the challenge of providing for oneself and one's family, but it is a necessary psychological leap for our emotional survival. We must move past distrust and blame to focus on strategies for healing the self and then the organizations that we work with, not for.

## PRESCRIPTIONS FOR PERSONAL HEALING

The prescriptions that follow have been carefully selected to facilitate the process of personal healing. They hold true for managers and nonmanagers, salaried and hourly workers, and those in government, business, industry, health care, not-for-profit agencies, and public and private educational institutions—anyone who works for a living. The prescriptions represent some of the "upside-down thinking" that I believe is necessary to revolutionize our work lives.

### Rx: Become Your Own Employer

When we shifted our livelihood from the farm to the factory, we went to work for an organization under its owners and bosses. By so doing we created an ethic in which workers were beholden to the companies that hired them. This is how worker dependence and codependence, discussed elsewhere in this book, were born. This culture of "working for," "working under," and "belonging to" is what paved the way for the phenomenon of the organization man.

Whether we work in someone else's organization or in our own business, we must face this simple fact: under the new contract of the age of technology and information, we have created an environment in which fickle customers with ever more demanding standards have virtually limitless choices in getting their needs met. In our competitive global economy, workers remain in organizations, or in business, as long as they add value. Customers remain loyal as long as they receive value. The implications for defining our workplaces and the way we manage and collaborate are many. For one thing, unless we are in an area that our business views as a "core competency," an area involving the company's technology or trade secrets, chances are good that our jobs can be outsourced to a vendor who can do them faster, better, and cheaper. To compete for one's job as a surviving manager or employee, a person will have to prove his or her worth to the organization so that outsourcing no longer looks so attractive.

I read somewhere that employees who get hired into Microsoft these days are hired into a project team, not a job. The implication is that they are being valued for their knowledge, skills, and creativity, which will be applied where it is needed. Once the goals of the project team are achieved, they may move on to another team, not another job. My friend Harry Pickens likens this to his experience as a freelance musician: "You are responsible for upskilling yourself as a free agent. You must be ready and willing to work with different teams at the drop of a hat. The person who hires the musician simply puts him or her in touch with the work team. It is the musicians' responsibility to make themselves marketable—to retrain and retool themselves."

In the culture of entitlement and codependence, to be a free agent was tantamount to failure. Becoming a self-employed free agent may now be the most important prescription for success. The healthiest employees will be those who take fuller responsibility for their employment. This is true whether one works inside an organization as a nurse, engineer, supervisor, or clerk or outside it as an entrepreneur. And it is truer now than at any time since the industrial revolution. Today, to truly survive and thrive, we must return to the notion of self-employment that served people in the agrarian society. We must let go of old notions of the job and embrace new ways of working and earning a living.

This is a difficult journey, for it means becoming an architect of our own future and a partner in revolutionizing the workplace. To achieve this, we must first recognize that "we are our organizations." In my earlier book, *Leadership: The Journey Inward,* I reminded my readers that "to transform our organizations, our communities or our lives, we must first transform ourselves." This transformation requires that we disengage from the past, taking its lessons. We must then squarely face the reality that things will never be the same. By freeing ourselves from illusions about our present situation, we can embrace its reality and work to change it. Having moved from denial and disillusionment, we free ourselves to create the future we envision. For employees this holds the key to our movement from dependence on and codependence with our organizations to independence and interdependence. We must move from working *for* our organizations to working *with* them to create a healthier economy and work environment. Only then can we unleash the personal power that drives transformational change, which brings me to the next prescription.

### Rx: Develop New Skills and Competencies

Adopting a self-employed perspective means that individual workers must take charge of their livelihoods and take responsibility for developing new skills and competencies to support their marketability. Many smart companies are turning to expanded training as a way to make themselves more competitive. As a survivor, an employee must aggressively seek out such opportunities and create new ones. My evening management classes at Carnegie Mellon University are filled with smart opportunists who are looking out for their future as a more marketable "business entity." In most cases their tuition is paid for or supplemented by the organizations for which they currently work. This is a win-win situation insofar as the organizations benefit from their enhanced skills and the students themselves become better positioned in the marketplace should they be excessed out of their present position.

These students are mostly full-time professionals and managers who come from such varied fields as city government, health care, not-for-profit agencies, business, and industry.

They include physicians, journalists, and attorneys as well as supervisors and managers—all seeking a degree in public policy and management with an eye to the future. For some this is a third or fourth professional degree. They have embraced the concept of lifelong learning and are willing to change their careers several times if need be to remain flexible and self-sustaining in their work lives. They report, by the way, tremendous personal benefits, such as enhanced self-esteem, feelings of empowerment, and a chance to be continuously on the leading edge of the latest technology and the latest information.

The healthiest workers I consult with in large downsizing companies are those who adopt this mind-set. They are vigorously seeking out the internal technical and interpersonal training offered by their companies. As one Westinghouse employee told me, "I feel that this way we both win. I keep my skills current and make myself marketable, while the company continues to get the best I have to offer."

Achieving mastery at whatever we do is one of the keys to success and to personal healing in our evolving organizations. It is also the key to becoming marketable self-empowered experts rather than "hired hands." This leads naturally to the next prescription.

### Rx: Become Comfortable with Being Uncomfortable

Personal healing begins with our willingness to let go of an entitlement mentality regarding work and to embrace change and uncertainty as part of the way things are for customers, stockholders, employers, employees, and suppliers. To persist in denial only aggravates the stress of living in a rapidly changing world. Instead of looking for comfort and predictability at work, we must develop an internal comfort level based on confidence and competence. We must get used to goal setting that goes hand in hand with contingency planning for the next change. We must move past the fear of loss of control associated with change and identify the opportunities for personal growth and development.

In one of my "Journey Inward" leadership retreats, a participant in her early thirties blurted out, "All I want is to have some certainty about the direction that my career will take. Is that too much to ask?" The group of five launched into a lively debate about whether that could ever be possible these days.

"That used to be the case years ago," one group member offered, "when the 'good ol' boys' established career paths and mentored young professionals and apprentices with their future in mind. I think you're being naive to expect that now."

"Well, I refuse to believe that I could have earned a master's degree from an Ivy League MBA program only to be told there's no future for me," the first woman replied.

"You may not even be relying on your MBA five years from now," I suggested, adding fuel to the controversy; "your organization or some other organization might call forth your value-added competence in an entirely different line of work if you're open to change."

In our current workplace belief system, "making it through the ranks," taking lateral moves to "learn the business," or "paying your dues" as a follower before you can expect to be a credible leader all speak to the positive value we place on the breadth and depth of worker experience. In this age of diversification and diversity, that will not change. How we get that breadth and depth will be redefined, however. Trend watchers now tell us about the "new careerists" who will be changing their occupations several times during their lifetimes as personal interests and marketplace and organizational needs change. To survive in the future means to embrace uncertainty, change, and the risk taking that change implies. We must be flexible and adaptive in our stance toward organizational life.

Admittedly, we all need a certain amount of security in our world; otherwise we would be perpetually anxious as human beings. There is no doubt that extreme insecurity is stressful and ultimately damages the psyche. On the other hand, extreme security can lead to codependence, complacency, and lethargy. In many instances organizational codependency has led us to believe in a sort of unwritten tenure, in which many employees over the years got paid and promoted for putting in time. In several companies I know mediocrity has been routinely rewarded. Performance reviews, when they occurred, were often merely a formality used to help justify salary increases but having little to do with who got ahead or who stayed behind. A senior executive in a utilities company recently confided, "For years we simply moved poor performers into someone else's department. Now the pendulum has swung in the opposite direction. People are being laid off in droves. Even competent workers could be gone tomorrow. Our employees are shell-shocked by this development."

Researchers like Joel Brockner who study survivor responses to downsizing suggest that moderate job insecurity is a better predictor of productivity than extremely high or extremely low job insecurity. But, as I suggested earlier, this security is going to have to take a different form. It cannot be based on codependence on organizations; it must come intrinsically from the worker.

### Rx: Embrace Computer Technology as a Key to the Future

"Computers are the pen and pencil of the nineties," says telecommunications expert Audley Williams. "It's now become a basic skill for workforce survival. It doesn't matter whether you are in the banking industry like me, or an auto mechanic. Last week I went to get my inspection sticker. The mechanic went to the computer, logged on, and pulled down a menu that allowed him to connect to the State of New York Department of Motor Vehicles computer in order to report whether my car passed the emissions tests or not."

We have evolved into a global village where more information has been produced in the past thirty years than during the previous five thousand. In this rapidly changing world information continues to double every five years, as does our technological capacity to produce information, goods, and services. This means that work—how we harness and apply our energy—must also change.

It is no small coincidence that the word "work" originated from the Greek word for "energy," *ergon*, which evolved into the Germanic *wergon*, the German and Dutch *werk*, and the English *work*. (It is also not a coincidence that to be "alive" is to be "energized.") Work is human energy. In recent history we have created "workplaces" to harness and use this human energy to transform resources such as capital, materials, and technology into goods, services, and profits. These workplaces, or organizations, house systems of workers arranged to perform tasks by using their talents and technology.

Computers are an extension of human energy. Once we see computers in this light, we can become energized in new ways as we explore the potential they hold to make our work more efficient and more effective in every field. I watch with great interest as health care workers in a local hospital with whom I consult use computer technology to improve patient care delivery. I am more than mildly intrigued by the clean, efficient, silent power of the sparsely populated manufacturing facilities in which I now consult. In the emerging workplace information power both enhances and replaces people power. But this need not be a fearsome realization if we remember that computers are mere extensions of human energy, created by humans in their quest to work smarter.

## Rx: Restore a Healthy Relationship with Work

People work. We work because it is primal. We work because we must to survive. We also work to celebrate ourselves and explore our talents as unique creations. Work is central to family life as a means of raising children, teaching values, and satisfying basic needs for food, clothing, and shelter. Work is the medium through which we build communities and through which we re-create ourselves. We have moved from hunting and gathering to farming and industry, from raw wilderness to big cities and global economies, with work at the center of our explorations. We have created communications systems, from hieroglyphics to the Internet, to record and facilitate our work. We have invented tools and processes—from Stone Age implements to farm equipment, from industrial machines to high technology—to enable us to work faster, better, and smarter.

I believe that, if left to our own devices, most of us would spend a lifetime pursuing work that is meaningful and fulfilling. Unfortunately, many people end up settling for less. They abdicate their own passions and inner drives, deferring to organizational mandates or to a sense of self defined by the job they are given by an organization. This sets people up to ultimately achieve less than they are capable of. It stifles our true nature and along with it, in many cases, our talents and creativity.

How did we come to a place where many spend the best part of their waking hours engaged in activities that are "just a job" and where workers are categorized as "victims" or "survivors" based on whether they have a job or not? Are the notions of work as primal, work as art, work as worship, work as an extension of human motives, work as community building elusive myths eclipsed by the need to work faster, better, and smarter in order to survive?

This quest to work faster, better, and smarter created the "job" two hundred years ago. Ironically, the same quest eliminates jobs as we reinvent the workplace of the nineties. But this may be a good thing, for, to truly survive our workplaces in this age of downsizing and restructuring, we will have to shift from our preoccupation with the job back to a focus on work itself.

Author and consultant Janet Hagberg, a training colleague during my years at Alcoa, captured the attention of a group of leadership trainees once when she announced, "I'm beginning to concentrate less on my job and more on my work." She went on to explain her position. A job, she claimed, is merely a collection of tasks, an artificial carving up of duties for the sake of efficiency. Work, on the other hand, is a natural, spiritual extension of the self, a path to self-mastery and meaning in our lives. She suggested that we should all be about the business of discovering our life's purpose through our work.

Later, a member of the class pulled me aside to express his skepticism. He dismissed her philosophy as a bit high-flown. Perhaps this was true for artists and musicians, he suggested, but not for the typical employee in the plant where he worked. That was ten years ago, but I am still reminded daily of that conversation, as clients who are burned-out survivors of downsizing bitterly confide, "I used to enjoy working here. But now this is just a job."

In his beautiful book *Artful Work*, Dick Richards convincingly makes the claim that in the industrial age science drove art, and with it meaning, out of work. We have indeed departed from the pre-Newtonian concept that "work well accomplished was art." As a culture we have made an unnatural split between what is useful or necessary and what is meaningful in our hearts and souls. This split has enabled leaders in some quarters to see humans as variable costs and work as something we do to make money, rather than as something primal to our existence as physical, mental, emotional, moral, and spiritual beings.

On a trip to Nassau several years ago, I was served by a waitress who sang while she worked. I said to her, "You're singing while you work. How nice! But why?"

She smiled and said, "It makes the day go easier." (I'd secretly hoped that she would say, "I love my job," but her response was still interesting to me.)

I recalled how growing up in Jamaica over forty years ago the men and women sang work songs. These were melodic chants punctuated with the rhythm of sledge hammers on stone as they built a house or paved a road. I later learned that work songs have long been a part of all indigenous cultures. In fact, in Africa work songs were sacred because work was sacred. There was no separation between the secular and the sacred, so that the use of song and music was functional: to teach basic skills, to teach culture, to record history, and, very importantly, to energize work. In my work as a seminar leader, my audiences are always energized when I speak of "finding our song through work."

The main dilemma for the survivors in restructured organizations becomes how to move, like the organization, from old employee expectations to something healthier, more reality based. The challenge of the survivor is how to get personal needs and motives in sync with the needs and motives of the organizations created to serve us. Eventually we must go "back to a future" in which work honors the soul of the worker. To survive we have to let go of the "it's-just-a-job" mentality and go back to the point at which workers are independent and interdependent purveyors of their skills and talents as they forge new relationships with the workplace. The organization itself will require this kind of worker if it is to survive.

### Rx: Reframe How You Think About Your Situation

"The mind has two parts, a thinker and a prover. Whatever we hold to be true, the mind sets out to create it as fact. In this way we preserve our sanity!" This is how a psychologist friend once described the relationship between our thoughts, feelings, and actions. We were having a discussion about the few people we meet in downsizing organizations who see the changes as heady, stimulating stuff. It has to do with reframing, she suggested. You have to be willing to look at the situation and say to yourself, What am I supposed to make of these challenges? If you frame the uncertainty as an opportunity to develop independence and to grow in new ways, you will be less stressed out and make more practical, lifesaving choices than if you simply focus on how bad things are.

I am struck by the fact that whenever I conduct organizational effectiveness surveys, whether in healthy companies or in companies in the throes of uncertainty and pain, participants have a lot more energy in response to my question What's the worst thing about working here? than to the next question, What's the best thing about working here? But I have also observed that the most satisfied workers are those who manage to engage in positive self-talk: At the end of the day, I feel I have made a difference in my customers' lives. They have a very different emotional experience than those whose only focus is Things are worse around here than they used to be.

I am reminded of an interview I conducted in 1990 with the Haitian artist Jean Fritz Chery. He was born with a serious physical disability, having no arms, just a small stump on one shoulder. In 1981, Chery won the United Nations International Year of the Handicapped Artist Award. He had risen to international prominence as an artist famous for his brightly hued paintings of fish—creatures he related to because they, too, had no arms but were able to function wonderfully in their habitat. Enthralled by Chery's positive outlook and his personal strength, I sought him out to learn his story. He explained to me that he had never viewed the absence of arms as a "handicap." Rather, he saw it as a condition that afforded him more possibilities. "When I get tired of painting with my mouth," he explained, "I shift to my left foot; when I'm tired of working with my left foot, I shift to my right foot. People with two arms and hands limit themselves. They only paint with one hand. And when that hand gets tired, they stop."

Unfortunately, the most difficult change to achieve is a change in mind-set. Few people in today's trying business times have learned the survival secret of reframing. Survivors' biggest challenge in charting a new social contract with their employees is moving from a focus on fear and blame to a focus on self-renewal. To hold on to negative thoughts about what is not working to the exclusion of positive thoughts about how to create personal change amounts to wasted energy in the new economy. People who engage in negative self-talk in the face of restructuring become immobilized by their own fears. This paralysis prevents them from moving competitively into a marketplace they see as frightening.

As human beings our inner urgings are to be free, secure, self-sufficient. The belief systems we were taught deny us the possibility of giving life to those urgings.

## *Rx: Create a Blended Work and Personal Life*

As the quality of our work life changes, it is useful to remember that work is an extension of our thoughts, our talents, our capabilities. We measure our competence and our self-worth by our ability to be effective (i.e., to achieve results) through our work as a parent, a carpenter, an engineer, a teacher, a manager, a waiter, a griot, an artist, or a governor.

In the industrial age the workplace became the center of human activity. Much of the attention and activities of schools, government, business, and industry focused on the workplace. The workweek reigned supreme over nonworkplace activities. Banking, reading utility meters, and most other services were predicated on the nine to five workweek. The traditional nuclear family was structured to enable the nine to five activities of business and commerce—the "real work." As larger and larger numbers of women entered the workforce, the centrality of the workplace became even more profound. It was not convenient for Johnny to get a fever in the middle of the workweek. It was certainly taboo to bring one's personal and family life issues to the workplace. One's personal and work life were to be compartmentalized. Work was "real life," and personal and family matters were not expected to intrude into this world of real work. Americans were expected to adapt family to the workplace, not vice versa. We became obsessively focused on our jobs, those neat units of activities created so that we could assign tasks, monitor and measure worker productivity, and set salaries more efficiently.

The routinized world of the nine to five job is now being challenged, not only as an affront to the family-work balance but also as an effective way to structure, grow, and preserve society. Flextime, job sharing, the Family and Medical Leave Act, twenty-four–hour banking, self-directed work teams, outsourcing, and a host of other activities portend these changes. My clients who fifteen years ago would never bring family or personal balance up as subjects in corporate meetings and training sessions now routinely raise these issues as they speak about work. Support groups for executives are springing up everywhere as these workers also meet to search for ways to find balance and meaning in their work lives.

The transformations we are creating in our world are attempts to heal our dis-ease. Clearly, there are forces afoot that are causing the tearing down of walls, the explosions and implosions of governments and businesses, and the falling apart and the coming together of diverse cultures. We hope that, phoenixlike out of the ashes of these paradoxes and seeming chaos, there will emerge a redefinition of our work and the relationships that support it.

# Conclusion

—✿—

# WHAT'S YOUR
# SURVIVOR PROFILE?

My observations and discussions with survivors and survivor managers have revealed that the primary motives determining how we see ourselves in relation to work also play an important role in determining how we perceive, feel, and act in the face of downsizing or other changes. When I counsel survivors, I often ask, "If you won the lottery and you still chose to work, what would motivate you to work? What motivates you now?" Drawing on their responses and guided by the work of career management specialists, I have identified and labeled nine categories of human work motives.

Assuming that most employees work to earn a living and that at some level, therefore, we are motivated by a need for money and security, let us look at the other motives that drive us to see how they shape our experience in a downsizing, restructuring, less-secure economy. Also keep in mind that each of us may be driven by one or more of the following types of motives at different points in our lives and in different situations. But we each have a "home base": the motive we would be most reluctant to give up if we had to make a choice.

**High achievers** are extremely driven. Their primary goal is to do more, be more successful, look good, move ahead. They are extremely goal oriented, and they work harder and harder to fulfill increasingly challenging ambitions. Some may not experience job satisfaction in their lifetime, but they still keep focused on achievement. Some high achievers are just driven, without really knowing why. Others are driven to achieve more and more money or status, because the amount of money they earn or the status they achieve is a measure of their worth in the marketplace and of their self-worth.

High achievers often face a real crisis of identity in the face of layoffs and restructuring. They are used to working their way out of challenging situations by trying harder, putting in more time and effort, and eventually getting rewarded for doing so. They are used to being valued and promoted, often into management, for their efforts. In the face of measures like reengineering, when the organization literally wipes the slate clean and starts over, they face the real possibility that other criteria may be more central than intensity and drive. They often have a difficult time coming to terms with the reality that they may not be able to simply work their way out of the situation by trying harder.

*Case in Point:* By all accounts Cathy Sturdivis was a high achiever. Without a college degree or much formal training in retailing, she had risen over a twelve-year period from salesclerk, to floor manager, to assistant buyer, to buyer. During this period she had given birth to twin boys and a daughter. She was a quick study, highly innovative, and extremely goal oriented. She logged long hours and attended every retail conference and workshop she could find, often financing her education with her own money. Her tenacity was rewarded with increasing responsibility and more challenging assignments. Her small, cluttered office was lined with awards and accolades from both the retail industry and her community, where she volunteered for social causes during her scanty spare time. With each promotion she began planning for the next.

When the news of a buyout of the department store chain where she worked came, Cathy's first question to the store manager was "How will this affect my career?" He couldn't give her a straight answer. No one really knew yet what the new owners planned to do. Rumors ran that under the new ownership the products would be inferior, that the acquired stores would be relocated to the Southern states, that their own store might be closed—or that it might be expanded. Cathy's response to the chaos of the transition was to work harder. Her goal was to impress the new owners with performance. If they saw what she could offer, they would likely retain her as part of the transition team. She also attempted to hedge her bets by circulating her résumé elsewhere, just in case the store closed.

Cathy's children saw less and less of her as she became immersed in working her way through the impending crisis. Her marriage fell apart. She ultimately left the store for a competing store at a higher salary, and she enrolled in college at night to continue her education. She loved her new job. Yet, she became consumed with guilt about her preoccupation with work, and she felt compelled to explain herself constantly or to apologize for her behavior.

When Cathy attended one of my weekend group sessions for "pioneer" women in business, she confided that throwing herself into the new job had helped her work through the crises of her divorce and of her career challenge. Like many of the high achievers in the support group, work had become a balm that provided relief from the stresses of her personal life.

Through these group sessions Cathy came to terms with the fact that her way of coping with the stress of an uncertain work environment was to become immersed in the work she loved. Rather than seeing this as a personality flaw, she began working toward creating a more blended life that included quality time for parenting, time for herself, and time for her work. She now realizes that some things must be sacrificed in order to achieve this. She has put night school on hold for a few years, until her children are older. She has also extended her circle of support to include the Big Brothers and Big Sisters programs for her children. In the meantime, she no longer apologizes to anyone for loving her work as an important part of her life both financially and spiritually.

**Entrepreneurs** are driven by a need to create and run a business of their own. But not all entrepreneurs realize this dream. Many spend their entire careers working inside government, business, or some other field. They may spend that time planning to leave one day, or they may secretly run a small business on the side, or they may find the necessary satisfaction and security in their job, especially if it is in an area such as research or marketing where they can satisfy their need to create and implement a business concept. But it is also important to entrepreneurs that they be recognized for their achievement. I have met entrepreneurial scientists, for example, who were pained by the fact that all their patents must be registered in the company's name. They frame the company's token dollar and plaque, given in recognition of their role in securing the patent, and hang this proudly in their living rooms for everyone to see.

The entrepreneurial worker can be valuable to organizations that are seeking to empower employees to make breakthrough innovations. Smart managers have provided some entrepreneurial workers seed money to start internal skunk works. The company benefits from generating new profit centers or new innovations. The employee benefits from satisfying his or her entrepreneurial needs, especially if compensation is tied to the results they get. Interestingly, the few entrepreneurial types I meet in business see downsizing as an opportunity to rise to the challenge of either striking out on their own or of helping management find innovative ways to revitalize the organization. Some even feel comfortable taking the risks of speaking up and championing their ideas as they try to influence top management.

*Case in Point:* In chapter 2 we met Dolores Williams, the colleague of my friend Maynard Coleman whose philosophy was to "quit before I'm laid off." For Dolores the announcement of her company's downsizing plans was nothing more than a rather welcome excuse to do what she had always wanted to do: buy a franchise and launch out on her own. As you will recall, she was a fast-tracker in an area declared "core" by the business and therefore had more job security than many of her colleagues. Like most employees, Dolores was never taught during her schooling to view entrepreneurship as a viable career alternative. Like most of us, she was programmed to get a job and work for someone else—preferably someone established and secure in the competitive marketplace.

Yet, Dolores harbored secret dreams of being a business owner. For years she subscribed to magazines like *Inc.*, *Success*, and *Entrepreneurial Woman*, losing herself in what was nothing more than a fantasy world of possibilities that others were living out while she worked in her respectable Fortune 500 job as a lab technician. She told me how surprised she was that the announcement of layoffs actually made her heart leap with joy. On following her feelings further, she became consumed with the ever present awareness that now was the time to take the plunge, while her courage was still full-blown.

Dolores had always been uncomfortable with the constraints of being a lab technician who could not innovate, who had to wait for directives from her supervisor, a senior scientist whose ideas she often felt lacked imagination. On several occasions they had experienced tensions while she second-guessed his suggestions, offering ideas that she thought were more creative. Reflecting on those times, she began to relish the idea of calling the shots and of creating a business that reflected her own notions. So she took her life savings, including her 401(k) retirement funds, and launched out on her own. And even though Dolores has run into hard times and had long, grueling hours, she has never looked back. She confides that now she has lived through the risk of starting a business she is virtually fearless. If her venture should fail, she insists, she would simply find another.

**Thrill seekers** seek the exhilaration of stunt work or the high that comes from conquering unsolvable projects. They typically move from experience to experience in search of greater stimulation, finding joy in each seemingly insurmountable challenge. Whether they wrestle alligators in the boggy waters of Florida or wrestle with problems in the corridors of corporate life, their work satisfaction comes from the rush of risk taking and the elation of conquering the unconquerable.

I once met a thrill seeker in a leadership course I conducted at Westinghouse. Participants were sharing their concerns about how that company's major transitions might affect them personally. The thrill seeker, who was also definitely the class "oddball" spoke up after a few minutes. He said, "I wish everyone would just quit whining; this could light a fire under people and cause us to rise to the occasion. I personally find the changes stimulating. It's like living on the edge."

*Case in Point:* Skip Taylor was always restless. He was brilliant at many different things, and those close to him reminded him that therein lay his problem: he could do anything he set his mind to really well, and he set his mind to a lot of different things. But the minute a project was up and running, he got bored with it and wanted to move on to the next venture. In his job as a sales manager for a group of specialty retail shops in Denver, he had launched many innovative projects, all of which continued to benefit the stores six years later. But he left the Denver stores after three years, not enough time to see any of his creative projects come to fruition.

Skip's next stint, as director of community relations for an HMO in New Jersey, was a stimulating change of pace. He had to learn a lot about health care very quickly. He had to establish new contacts in a community in which he had never lived. The HMO was growing rapidly and could barely keep pace with its growing clientele. His charge was to make sure that customer service and the HMO's image did not suffer during its rapid growth period. He instituted several important outreach initiatives that solidified the HMO's position in the marketplace.

Just as Skip's job was becoming routine (he felt that he had learned all he could for now and that he was no longer grappling with unsurmountable challenges), the HMO announced plans for a merger with another organization. This would mean restructuring and the loss of several jobs. His colleagues were thrown into deep despair. How could they have gone so rapidly from dramatic growth to layoffs? The high energy of success was quickly replaced by the shock, disbelief,

and pain typically expected in the wake of such pronounce-
ments.

As people milled around daily lamenting the impending
losses, Skip pretended to care, while he secretly hoped that his
job would be on the cutting block. He was ready to move on,
but he didn't want his résumé to reveal his restlessness for new
adventures. If he were laid off because of a merger, it would
look better on his employment history, which already was beginning to reveal a string of two- to three-year stints. If he were
among the downsized employees, he could save face while being freed up to seek his next career thrill.

**Creatives** work to express their ideas and creativity.
Whether they chose to be a bricklayer or a musician, first grade
teacher or engineer, artisan or novice, their work is their worship—a celebration of the talents they embody or the beauty
they experience in the universe. They can get lost in their work
for countless hours. Time stands still as they become one with
their art or their craft. There are no boundaries between themselves and their work. Modern-day philosophers teach us, "Do
what you love and the money will follow."

Those for whom work is worship often profit from their
work, but not always. Like entrepreneurs, the creatives I meet
in downsizing organizations focus their energies on figuring
out how to continue to practice their craft internally or externally. But unlike the specialists or the security seekers (whom
I'll discuss later), creatives willingly go wherever they are sent
as long as they can continue to do work that is meaningful to
them.

*Case in Point:* Chris Kim's most profound connection with
school was that it allowed him to lose himself in art. He
ultimately earned degrees in design and engineering from a
prestigious university and landed a position with an auto manufacturer. In no time he became a leading designer turning out
well-received concepts on paper for a line of cars.

When his company announced plans to cut ten thousand
jobs, Chris, a rather quiet and reticent person, had very little to
say. He lost himself in his work, as he always had. I met his

wife, a former student of mine, for lunch one day and inquired how her husband was doing. "Oh, I'm not sure," she said. "His company has announced a major layoff, but he isn't taking my advice to get his résumé out there. He seems preoccupied. And he's been shopping a lot lately."

I was surprised at this last comment. Chris wasn't into clothes or things. I couldn't even picture him shopping. On probing this further, I learned that he had begun to purchase more and more art supplies, an expanded workstation, a state-of-the-art computer, and the best design software applications available—all for his studio at home, where he was spending longer hours consumed in creating new design ideas outside his industry interests. While he wasn't circulating his résumé widely, in his own way he was expanding his repertoire and increasing the likelihood that he would be well positioned to continue his creative pursuits in whatever form they might take and wherever they might take him.

It turns out that Chris did not lose his job at the auto manufacturer. But he lived through the crisis of downsizing without ever having experienced the pains of survivor syndrome. He was too consumed in his creative world to be assaulted by the uncertainty and fears most survivors face.

**Caretakers** are dedicated to serving humanity. No matter what profession they choose or what job they land, they are motivated to use it to support, enable, or heal others. Whether they become a nurse or a soldier, homemaker or attorney, physician or environmentalist, politician or engineer, work has meaning to them only if they experience it as contributing to the goodwill of humanity and the planet. The caretaker on the assembly line is not only aware of the needs of everyone around him or her but is also deeply aware of and concerned about the end users' needs. The caretaker joins the Peace Corps for different reasons than the thrill seeker, who wants adventure. The caretaker joins the Peace Corps to change the world.

The stress level experienced by caretakers in downsizing organizations can be awesome. They sympathize deeply with those who leave and empathize fully with those who remain. Their attention turns to helping others grieve, heal, and find comfort. Yet, their anger and mistrust of the leadership can be quite potent. A caretaker at AT&T confided, "I spend so much time taking care of everyone's feelings and needs around here, I have little energy left to take care of me and my family at the end of the day."

*Case in Point:* When her business unit was cut by 30 percent, Mariella Conti telephoned me to ask for advice. "My office is like Grand Central Station," she announced. "People are dropping in all day to vent their frustrations, and I can't get my work done. I started coming in at 6:30 to get some work in before others arrived. Somehow word got out, [and] now people are calling me early mornings from their car phones as they commute to work!"

Mariella is not a human resources counselor. She is not the company's employee assistance program representative. She is actually a computer programmer who manages information systems at a home appliances manufacturer. All through school she excelled at computers. She loved the field with a passion. Her greatest concern when she entered the workforce five years earlier, however, had been that she not be stereotyped as a computer jock, locked away behind the scenes with little interpersonal contact.

Mariella had worked her way through undergraduate and graduate school in not-for-profit organizations that, in her words, allowed her to "serve others in meaningful ways." She later taught an introductory computer course at the local community college two nights a week to earn extra money to help her younger sisters pay for college expenses.

A classic caretaker, Mariella was loved and sought out by everyone at work. She stopped whatever she was doing to listen and lend support as coworkers casually dropped in for a chat throughout the day. Needless to say, with the announcement of downsizing, this only intensified, as potential victims and potential survivors alike came to see her office as a place where they would get unconditional support as they vented their fears and frustrations. Interestingly, she advised many people how to prepare for the cuts, but found little time to think about the possible impact on her own career or to explore personal options.

Through our discussions Mariella has come to understand her challenge: how to manage her personal and professional boundaries so that she can remain true to her loving, giving nature while also taking care of herself. She has begun to block out time on her calendar for personal needs. She is also experimenting with closing her door for an hour or two each day, but, true to form, she posts a carefully worded, apologetic Please Do Not Disturb sign on her door. Underneath the smiley face at the top, the plaque reads "Please understand my brief 'closed-door' policy. I need to concentrate for a while. I'll be available again at. . . ." The makeshift hands of a clock at the bottom of the plaque indicate the time when she will reopen the door.

**Mavericks** approach work governed by their need to assert their individuality and independence. They seek freedom from the constraints of organizational mandates and the nine to five routine. They may of necessity hire into an organization, but they are truly satisfied only if it allows them flexibility and self-sufficiency. These nonconforming individualists are sometimes seen as radical—they insist on telling the truth as they see it. They are often sought out for their alternative views and their willingness to challenge the status quo or to counsel people who are in transition. At their best, mavericks are positive warrior-healers and agents of change. At their worst, they are troublesome rabble-rousers. Many of my colleagues who are college professors, "alternative" therapists, management consultants, and visionary leaders fit this mold.

I have a lot of fun with the mavericks in my client organizations that have reduced their workforce and restructured. They are almost always righteously indignant: "They don't know what they're doing." "I saw this coming." "Corporate leaders are confused." They are filled with radical solutions and outline them to whoever will listen. It's as if they finally feel vindicated for having lived "outside the box" all along. I don't worry much about mavericks; because they embody many of the qualities that emerging organizations seek, they tend to land on their feet.

*Case in Point:* When I met Don Reid, he had been transferred to corporate headquarters from his job as plant superintendent at a major aircraft products manufacturer. His reputation was legendary. In a company where most employees feared reprisals for bucking the system, he was outspoken and fearless. When the CEO came to his plant for routine visits, he was the vocal front man, even before he moved into management. He would ask the tough questions with a tone of "What are you guys up to anyway?" Then he would launch into his stance of "Well, here's how I see it." His ideas were brilliant. His grasp of the industry was better than most. Although the senior managers never told him so publicly, they found his ideas provocative and very useful.

When his company experienced a major shake-up that resulted in a de-layering of management, the loss of fifteen hundred jobs, and the installation of a new CEO, Don was in his element. He had seen it coming—had predicted it four years earlier and no one had believed him. Now he had some ideas on the necessary next steps. He voiced these during a plant visit by the new CEO, and then followed up with a copious fifty-page memo addressed to senior management at the corporate headquarters. Their response shocked the plant. Corporate invited Don to the Chicago headquarters for a weeklong visit that culminated in a job offer: vice president for organizational development.

It was a big gamble and a major investment, but the new CEO and his staff were convinced that what they needed was a maverick who could champion outside-the-box thinking and bring the plant perspective to the corporate offices. As part of his grooming, they sent Don to National Training Labs for intensive work in organizational development and then to an eight-week Ivy League management program. Don is making major inroads in his new position. Among other things, he has installed a training and counseling program for the survivors of downsizing.

**Directors** are motivated by being in charge. They are most fulfilled when they get to take the lead. They like to combine resources and their problem-solving skills to direct the activities of others toward some goal. Whether or not they become the formally designated supervisor or manager, these workers prefer to direct and control the performance of work activities. (Those who take management jobs solely for motives such as money or status often experience great stress in our emerging workplace if they don't find strategic problem solving and the task of leading others satisfying.) Directors spend longer and longer hours strategizing when their organization is in transition. They relentlessly apply their problem-solving and interpersonal skills to the business of figuring out how to revitalize the organization. If they are not in a formal management or supervisory position, they constantly seek the ear of managers, offering their tactical plans and directives.

*Case in Point:* Cynthia Howell works as the marketing representative for a small cosmetics chain. She had previously worked as a project manager in a Fortune 500 company, a job she reluctantly gave up to return home to Pittsburgh to care for her ailing mother. In her previous job she had also been a total quality management facilitator and had enjoyed great success as part of the company's Quality Council, the group charged with championing and implementing the TQM efforts.

Cynthia's new job with the cosmetics firm was a step down careerwise, but she was comfortable with it for the short term. It had opened up new learning opportunities and provided a fairly good income while she supported her mother. The only drawback was that she could no longer apply her expertise as a manager. No one reported to her, something she really missed. In addition, her new company was restructuring and eliminating jobs. She was relatively sure that her position would not be affected, but she was rather frustrated about not having a role to play in how this transition got managed. In fact, she was becoming increasingly aware of feeling out of control as the changes were being implemented.

Cynthia has taken to furiously doodling flowcharts and diagrams of interrelationships and processes during business meetings. She then leans over to whoever will listen and leads sidebar conversations about what managers need to do to engage survivors and stimulate profits. This is becoming disruptive, and her supervisor recently called her aside after a meeting to ask her to cut down on the distracting chatter. In the conversation that ensued Cynthia shared her frustration and reminded her supervisor that she had had great experience managing the implementation of change. Luckily for Cynthia, her supervisor was not threatened by these concerns. They began exploring ways that Cynthia's career path could move more rapidly toward management. In the meantime, Cynthia meets regularly for informal lunches with her supervisor to brainstorm and share ideas. For now, this director has found an outlet for her leadership inclinations, even though she is currently not supervising a staff of her own.

**Specialists** are "occupation bound"; that is, they seek work that allows them to focus exclusively on their field of expertise. Edgar Schein describes this type of worker as the modern equivalent of the craftsman. In his landmark work *Career Anchors*, Schein labels what motivates this worker as "technical/ functional competence." Such workers would not relish being asked to give up their practice as, say, an accountant or master plumber in order to supervise people outside their fields. They might take a supervisory job if it were related to their area of technical competence, or they might, like a research scientist I know, decline supervision of others altogether in order to remain immersed in their craft.

There is another kind of specialist, the everyday employee who complacently insists when asked to do something different, "That's not my job." Because specialists are bound to their identity as senior engineer or second-shift mechanic, or by their job description, they easily fall into the codependent trap.

This is because they inflexibly look to the organization to provide them a job in their chosen vocation or to provide fixed boundaries regarding their job. Some may even become victims of layoffs because they refuse to explore other avenues of work in the organization.

*Case in Point:* Maynard Coleman, the engineer profiled in chapter 2, is a classic example of the specialist. He decided as a child that he wanted to work in space exploration as an engineer. His choices followed that intention throughout his schooling and into his career. He is now deeply immersed in his field, his core identity shaped by his professional affiliation. He sees work as his "calling" and could not imagine pursuing a different occupation.

As discussed earlier, the depression he experienced in response to his company's announcement of downsizing plans was linked to his dependence on an organization that might or might not allow him to play out his life-defining career aspirations. In retrospect, it seems that his temporary despair could also have been tied to the various motivations that rage in an internal battle in his psyche.

While Maynard's primary style is as a specialist, he has integrated other secondary motivations as well. As a specialist he needs the assurance of a place in his field, but he is also a unique combination of thrill seeker and high achiever. The specialist as thrill seeker enjoys the high of conquering "unsolvable" scientific challenges. The specialist as high achiever has made himself invaluable to the company in a core competency area and continues to outperform the best.

In addition, because Maynard was able to work through his fears and embrace training and other strategies to hedge his bets and rebuild his self-esteem, there is little doubt that he will continue to find success either in his present company or elsewhere if he has to. In these respects Coleman is more fortunate than the many specialists in downsizing organizations who are unable to get in touch with their other motives and drives and find ways to create alternative choices.

**Security seekers** embody the potential to be among the unhappiest survivors in downsizing organizations. While all workers need some degree of security, security seekers hold job security as their primary work motive. Above all else they seek employment or a trade or profession that guarantees stability and predictability. They gain their sense of well-being from affiliation. For these workers "making it" means that they are vested and tenured in their organizations. Like their forefather, the organization man, they are bound to the notion of a job for life. They forgo the heady risk taking that thrill seekers or entrepreneurial workers crave. They seek direction from their supervisors and job descriptions rather than challenging the status quo or championing radical innovations. They are reluctant to move outside their field, their company, or their comfort zone. Security seekers are also bound in powerless codependence with their company or union, but for a particular reason. They entrust their future to and derive their sense of self from affiliation with their organization. They expect protection in return for their loyalty.

Security seekers in today's rapidly changing, shrinking organizations find themselves grappling with very different assumptions about work and the workplace than their parents did. Unfortunately, many are stuck in denial, holding on to the possibility that things might, or ought to, return to the way they were. Unless they find ways to break their chains of codependence, security seekers have great difficulty adjusting in the new workplace.

*Case in Point:* On graduating from high school, John Milner entered college and joined the Army Reserve Officers Training Corps (ROTC) program. He felt good about his decision. He had lost an older brother in the Vietnam War, but he harbored no ill feelings toward the military. He had always known that as an enlisted man he could gain educational benefits and carve out a secure future for himself. Upon graduating from college he was stationed at Fort Bragg, North Carolina, where he worked in human resources for four years. He was later transferred to the West Coast, where he spent fifteen years in successively responsible jobs. After retiring from the army at age thirty-nine with a full pension, he achieved another lifelong dream. He returned to his hometown of Atlanta to be near his family. His children were growing up without the benefit of the extended family relationships he had been used to as a child. John believed in the importance of being what he called "rooted," whether he spoke of family relationships or career.

Back in Atlanta, John secured a job with the Department of Veterans Affairs as a benefits coordinator. The pay was adequate, the benefits were excellent, and the job was secure. When the federal government furloughed "nonessential" workers, he was among them. Even though he continued to receive his salary and even though he knew that it was a temporary interruption in his work, he was devastated by the experience. For the first time he became acutely aware of his organization man mentality. He began reflecting on his life and career and came to the realization that every move he had made in the military and now in his civilian government job was determined for him by someone else.

John fell into deep despair and could not concentrate or function effectively when he returned to work. His anxiety increased, and his fears about the future became increasingly obsessive and unrealistic. At the insistence of his wife, he has begun to receive counseling from a psychotherapist. He hopes that through this process he will come to realize the value of the other safety nets in his life. These include the pension he has already earned, the fact that his wife now runs a successful day care center, and the fact that he has valuable, marketable skills and experiences that are transferable to other kinds of work.

# *Appendix*

—∿∿—

# SURVIVOR PROFILE QUIZ

In the space to the right of each statement, circle the appropriate number to indicate the degree to which the statement is true for you. Use the following scale:

1 = never true
2 = rarely true
3 = sometimes true
4 = often true
5 = always true

|  | Never | | | | Always |
|---|---|---|---|---|---|

1. I enjoy competing to do, or be, the best at work.  1 2 3 4 5
2. I like the idea of running my own business.  1 2 3 4 5
3. I love solving tough, "unsolvable" problems.  1 2 3 4 5
4. I tend to see things "differently" from most people at work.  1 2 3 4 5
5. I am happiest in a job where I can use my people skills to serve others.  1 2 3 4 5
6. If I leave my current job, I believe that I would easily land on my feet.  1 2 3 4 5
7. I like (or would like) being in charge of a whole organization.  1 2 3 4 5
8. I am committed to the field I have specialized in.  1 2 3 4 5
9. I need a job that provides lasting security.  1 2 3 4 5
10. I play to win.  1 2 3 4 5
11. It is important to me to create a product or service of my own.  1 2 3 4 5

|  |  | Never | Always |
|--|--|-------|--------|
| 12. | I am a risk taker. | | 1 2 3 4 5 |
| 13. | Friends, family, or colleagues tell me that I am creative. | | 1 2 3 4 5 |
| 14. | I enjoy helping others. | | 1 2 3 4 5 |
| 15. | I am happiest when I am unsupervised. | | 1 2 3 4 5 |
| 16. | I enjoy being in a leadership role. | | 1 2 3 4 5 |
| 17. | I want to build my career around what I know best. | | 1 2 3 4 5 |
| 18. | I would rather remain in a secure job with a fairly good salary and benefits than take a less secure job with excellent salary and benefits. | | 1 2 3 4 5 |
| 19. | I measure my career success by promotions and raises. | | 1 2 3 4 5 |
| 20. | I often think about ideas for starting my own business. | | 1 2 3 4 5 |
| 21. | I am always looking for the next challenge or project. | | 1 2 3 4 5 |
| 22. | I need freedom to express my creativity. | | 1 2 3 4 5 |
| 23. | I am willing to interrupt my daily tasks to help colleagues who stop by. | | 1 2 3 4 5 |
| 24. | I tell the truth as I see it at work, even if it's risky. | | 1 2 3 4 5 |
| 25. | I am most productive when I am in charge. | | 1 2 3 4 5 |
| 26. | I don't like having to do work that is not in my job description. | | 1 2 3 4 5 |
| 27. | I believe that organizations should seek to provide a "job for life." | | 1 2 3 4 5 |
| 28. | I like to be recognized for my accomplishments. | | 1 2 3 4 5 |
| 29. | I plan to be self-employed one day. | | 1 2 3 4 5 |
| 30. | The changes in my company do not scare me. | | 1 2 3 4 5 |
| 31. | I am aware of my talents and seek outlets for these talents. | | 1 2 3 4 5 |
| 32. | I sometimes take better care of others than of myself. | | 1 2 3 4 5 |
| 33. | I feel like I don't fit in at work. | | 1 2 3 4 5 |
| 34. | I seek out opportunities to solve problems and influence outcomes. | | 1 2 3 4 5 |
| 35. | I consider myself a specialist. | | 1 2 3 4 5 |
| 36. | I would rather follow than lead. | | 1 2 3 4 5 |
| 37. | I am more results oriented than most people. | | 1 2 3 4 5 |

|  | | Never | Always |
|---|---|---|---|
| | | 1 2 3 4 5 | |

38. I would like the freedom to create something that "has my name on it."      1 2 3 4 5

39. I find change and new directions stimulating.      1 2 3 4 5

40. I am (or would be) unhappy working in a job that doesn't require creativity.      1 2 3 4 5

41. My ideal career is one that allows me to help an important social cause.      1 2 3 4 5

42. I find rules and procedures to be stifling.      1 2 3 4 5

43. My goal is to secure (or remain) in a supervisory position.      1 2 3 4 5

44. I like the field I am in.      1 2 3 4 5

45. I don't like surprises or sudden changes in plans.      1 2 3 4 5

## SCORING YOUR SURVIVOR PROFILE

Transfer the numbers you circled to the corresponding spaces below. Then total your scores in each column to discover your preferences. How consistent are your scores with your current work situation? What can you do to make sure that there is more of a match between what you value and how you currently approach work?

| High achievers | Entrepreneurs | Thrill seekers | Creatives | Caretakers | Mavericks | Directors | Specialists | Security seekers |
|---|---|---|---|---|---|---|---|---|
| 1____ | 2____ | 3____ | 4____ | 5____ | 6____ | 7____ | 8____ | 9____ |
| 10____ | 11____ | 12____ | 13____ | 14____ | 15____ | 16____ | 17____ | 18____ |
| 19____ | 20____ | 21____ | 22____ | 23____ | 24____ | 25____ | 26____ | 27____ |
| 28____ | 29____ | 30____ | 31____ | 32____ | 33____ | 34____ | 35____ | 36____ |
| 37____ | 38____ | 39____ | 40____ | 41____ | 42____ | 43____ | 44____ | 45____ |
| Totals: | | | | | | | | |
| ____ | ____ | ____ | ____ | ____ | ____ | ____ | ____ | ____ |

NOTES:

# SELECTED READINGS

Bardwick, Judith M. *Danger in the Comfort Zone: From Boardroom to Mailroom—How to Break the Entitlement Habit That's Killing American Business*. New York: AMACOM, 1991.

Bridges, William. *JobShift: How to Prosper in a Workplace Without Jobs*. Reading, Mass.: Addison-Wesley, 1993.

———. *Managing Transitions: Making the Most of Change*. Reading, Mass.: Addison-Wesley, 1991.

———. *Surviving Corporate Transition: Rational Management in a World of Mergers, Layoffs, Start-ups, Takeovers, Divestitures, Deregulations, and New Technologies*. New York: Doubleday, 1988.

———. *Transitions: Making Sense of Life's Changes*. Reading, Mass.: Addison-Wesley, 1980.

Brockner, Joel, Mary Konovsky, Rochelle Cooper-Schneider, and Robert Folger. "Interactive Effects of Procedural Justice and Outcome Negativity on Victims and Survivors of Job Loss." *Academy of Management Journal* 37, no. 2 (April 1994): 397–409.

Cameron, Kim S. "Strategies for Successful Organizational Downsizing." *Human Resource Management* 33, no. 2 (summer 1994): 189.

Caudron, Shari. "Teach Downsizing Survivors How to Thrive." *Personnel Journal*, January 1996, 38.

Champy, James. *Reengineering Management*. New York: HarperBusiness, 1995.

Chawla, Sarita, and John Renesch, eds. *Learning Organizations*. Portland, Oreg.: Productivity Press, 1995.

Clark, Jim, and Richard Koonce. "Engaging Organizational Survivors." *Training & Development*, August 1995, 23.

Dent, Harry S., Jr. *Job Shock: Four New Principles Transforming Our Work and Business.* New York: St. Martin's Press, 1995.

Downs, Alan. *Corporate Executions: The Ugly Truth About Layoffs— How Corporate Greed Is Shattering Lives, Companies, and Communities.* New York: AMACOM, 1995.

Hagberg, Janet. *Real Power: The Stages of Personal Power in Organizations.* Salem, Wis.: Sheffield, 1994.

Hakim, Cliff. *We Are All Self-Employed: The New Social Contract for Working in a Changed World.* San Francisco: Berrett-Koehler, 1994.

Hammer, Michael, and James Champy. *Reengineering the Corporation.* New York: HarperCollins, 1993.

Handy, Charles. *The Age of Unreason.* London: Hutchinson, 1989.

Johansen, Robert, and Rob Swigart. *Upsizing the Individual in the Downsized Organization: Managing in the Wake of Reengineering, Globalization, and Overwhelming Technological Change.* Reading, Mass.: Addison-Wesley, 1994.

Kanter, Rosabeth Moss. *When Giants Learn to Dance: Mastering the Challenges of Strategy, Management, and Careers in the 1990s.* New York: Simon & Schuster, 1989.

Knowdell, Richard L., Elizabeth Branstead, and Milan Moravec. *From Downsizing to Recovery: Strategic Transition Options for Organizations and Individuals.* Palo Alto, Calif.: CPP Books, 1994.

Kübler-Ross, Elisabeth, and M. Warshaw. *Working It Through.* New York: Macmillan, 1969.

Lee, Chris. "After the Cuts." *Training,* July 1992, 17.

Merry, Martin D., and Donna Singer. "Healing the Healers." *Healthcare Forum* 37, no. 6 (November/December 1994): 37–41.

Mone, Mark A. "Relationships Between Self-Concepts, Aspirations, Emotional Responses, and Intent to Leave a Downsizing Organization." *Human Resource Management* 33, no. 2 (summer 1994): 281–98.

Moskal, Brian S. "Managing Survivors." *Industry Week,* August 3, 1992, 15.

Naisbitt, John, and Patricia Aburdene. *Re-inventing the Corporation: Transforming Your Job and Your Company for the New Information Society.* New York: Warner Books, 1985.

Navran, Frank J. *Truth & Trust: The First Two Victims of Downsizing.* Edmonton, Alberta, Canada: Athabasca University Educational Enterprises, 1995.

Noer, David M. *Healing the Wounds: Overcoming the Trauma of Layoffs and Revitalizing Downsized Organizations.* San Francisco: Jossey-Bass, 1993.

Rosenbluth, Hal F., and Diane McFerrin Peters. *The Customer Comes Second (And Other Secrets of Exceptional Service)*. New York: William Morrow, 1992.

Shechtman, Morris R. *Working Without a Net: How to Survive & Thrive in Today's High-Risk Business World*. New York: Pocket Books, 1994.

Siebert, Al. *The Survivor Personality*. Portland, Oreg.: Practical Psychology Press, 1994.

Smith, Lee. "Burned-Out Bosses." *Fortune*, July 25, 1994, 44.

Wexley, Kenneth, and Stanley Silverman. *Working Scared: Achieving Success in Trying Times*. San Francisco: Jossey-Bass, 1993.

# INDEX